T0233246

Lecture Notes in Computer Science   **9488**

Commenced Publication in 1973
Founding and Former Series Editors:
Gerhard Goos, Juris Hartmanis, and Jan van Leeuwen

Editorial Board

David Hutchison
  Lancaster University, Lancaster, UK
Takeo Kanade
  Carnegie Mellon University, Pittsburgh, PA, USA
Josef Kittler
  University of Surrey, Guildford, UK
Jon M. Kleinberg
  Cornell University, Ithaca, NY, USA
Friedemann Mattern
  ETH Zurich, Zürich, Switzerland
John C. Mitchell
  Stanford University, Stanford, CA, USA
Moni Naor
  Weizmann Institute of Science, Rehovot, Israel
C. Pandu Rangan
  Indian Institute of Technology, Madras, India
Bernhard Steffen
  TU Dortmund University, Dortmund, Germany
Demetri Terzopoulos
  University of California, Los Angeles, CA, USA
Doug Tygar
  University of California, Berkeley, CA, USA
Gerhard Weikum
  Max Planck Institute for Informatics, Saarbrücken, Germany

More information about this series at http://www.springer.com/series/7408

Fredrik Seehusen · Michael Felderer
Jürgen Großmann · Marc-Florian Wendland (Eds.)

Risk Assessment and Risk-Driven Testing

Third International Workshop, RISK 2015
Berlin, Germany, June 15, 2015
Revised Selected Papers

 Springer

Editors

Fredrik Seehusen
SINTEF ICT
Oslo
Norway

Michael Felderer
Institut für Informatik
Universität Innsbruck
Innsbruck
Austria

Jürgen Großmann
Fraunhofer Institut FOKUS
Berlin
Germany

Marc-Florian Wendland
Fraunhofer Institut FOKUS
Berlin
Germany

ISSN 0302-9743   ISSN 1611-3349   (electronic)
Lecture Notes in Computer Science
ISBN 978-3-319-26415-8   ISBN 978-3-319-26416-5   (eBook)
DOI 10.1007/978-3-319-26416-5

Library of Congress Control Number: 2015953793

LNCS Sublibrary: SL2 – Programming and Software Engineering

Springer Cham Heidelberg New York Dordrecht London

© Springer International Publishing Switzerland 2015
This work is subject to copyright. All rights are reserved by the Publisher, whether the whole or part of the material is concerned, specifically the rights of translation, reprinting, reuse of illustrations, recitation, broadcasting, reproduction on microfilms or in any other physical way, and transmission or information storage and retrieval, electronic adaptation, computer software, or by similar or dissimilar methodology now known or hereafter developed.
The use of general descriptive names, registered names, trademarks, service marks, etc. in this publication does not imply, even in the absence of a specific statement, that such names are exempt from the relevant protective laws and regulations and therefore free for general use.
The publisher, the authors and the editors are safe to assume that the advice and information in this book are believed to be true and accurate at the date of publication. Neither the publisher nor the authors or the editors give a warranty, express or implied, with respect to the material contained herein or for any errors or omissions that may have been made.

Printed on acid-free paper

Springer International Publishing AG Switzerland is part of Springer Science+Business Media
(www.springer.com)

Preface

The continuous rise of software complexity with increased functionality and accessibility of software and electronic components leads to an ever-growing demand for techniques to ensure software quality, dependability, safety, and security. The risk that software systems do not meet their intended level of quality can have a severe impact on vendors, customers, and even — when it comes to critical systems and infrastructures — daily life. The precise understanding of risks, as well as the focused treatment of risks, has become one of the cornerstones for critical decision making within complex social and technical environments. A systematic and capable risk and quality assessment program and its tight integration within the software development life cycle are key to building and maintaining secure and dependable software-based infrastructures.

This volume contains the proceedings of the Third International Workshop on Risk Assessment and Risk-Driven Testing (RISK 2015) held in June 2015 in Berlin, Germany, in conjunction with the OMG Technical Meeting, June 15–19, 2015. The workshop brought together researchers from the European Union to address systematic approaches combining risk assessment and testing. During the workshop, eight peer-reviewed papers were presented and actively discussed. The workshop was structured into three sessions namely: "Risk Assessment," "Risk and Development," and "Security Testing." The program was completed by a keynote on "Fundamental Principles of Safety Assurance" from Prof. Tim Kelly.

Owing to its integration with the OMG Technical Meeting, the workshop initiated a fruitful discussion between participants from industry and academia.

We would like to take this opportunity to thank the people who contributed to the RISK 2015 workshop. We want to thank all authors and reviewers for their valuable contributions, and we wish them a successful continuation of their work in this area.

September 2015

Jürgen Großmann
Marc-Florian Wendland
Fredrik Seehusen
Michael Felderer

Organization

RISK 2015 was organized by Fraunhofer FOKUS, SINTEF ICT, and the University of Innsbruck.

Organizing Committee

Jürgen Großmann	Fraunhofer FOKUS, Germany
Marc-Florian Wendland	Fraunhofer FOKUS, Germany
Fredrik Seehusen	SINTEF ICT, Norway
Michael Felderer	University of Innsbruck, Austria

Program Committee

Fredrik Seehusen	SINTEF ICT, Norway
Michael Felderer	University of Innsbruck, Austria
Jürgen Großmann	Fraunhofer FOKUS, Germany
Marc-Florian Wendland	Fraunhofer FOKUS, Germany
Ina Schieferdecker	FU Berlin/Fraunhofer FOKUS, Germany
Ketil Stølen	SINTEF ICT, Norway
Ruth Breu	University of Innsbruck, Austria
Ron Kenett	KPA Ltd. and University of Turin, Italy
Sardar Muhammad Sulaman	Lund University, Sweden
Bruno Legeard	University of Franche-Comté, France
Gabriella Carrozza	SELEX ES, Italy
Shukat Ali	Simula Research Laboratory, Norway
Markus Schacher	KnowGravity Inc., Switzerland
Alessandra Bagnato	Softeam, France
Kenji Taguchi	AIST, Japan
Zhen Ru Dai	University of Applied Science Hamburg, Germany
Tim Kelly	University of York, UK

Contents

Risk Assessment

Risk Assessment and Security Testing of Large Scale Networked Systems with RACOMAT

Johannes Viehmann[1(✉)] and Frank Werner[2]

[1] Fraunhofer FOKUS, Berlin, Germany
Johannes.Viehmann@fokus.fraunhofer.de
[2] Software AG, Darmstadt, Germany
Frank.Werner@softwareag.com

Abstract. Risk management is an important part of the software quality management because security issues can result in big economical losses and even worse legal consequences. While risk assessment as the base for any risk treatment is widely regarded to be important, doing a risk assessment itself remains a challenge especially for complex large scaled networked systems. This paper presents an ongoing case study in which such a system is assessed. In order to deal with the challenges from that case study, the RACOMAT method and the RACOMAT tool for compositional risk assessment closely combined with security testing and incident simulation for have been developed with the goal to reach a new level of automation results in risk assessment.

Keywords: Risk assessment · Security testing · Incident simulation

1 Introduction

For software vendors risk assessment is a big challenge due to the steadily increasing complexity of today's industrial software development and rising risk awareness on the customer side. Typically, IT systems and software applications are distributed logically and geographically, and encompass hundreds of installations, servers, and processing nodes. As customers rely on mature and ready-to-use software, products should not expose vulnerabilities, but reflect the state of the art technology and obey security risks or technical risks. Failing to meet customer expectations will result in a loss of customer trust, customer exodus, financial losses, and in many cases in legal consequences and law suits.

On the other hand, the impossibility to analyze and treat every potential security problem in advance is well-known. Any security issue without appropriate safeguards could lead to a considerable damage for the customer, be it its loss of business (e.g. when a successful DoS attack prevents business processes form being pursued), loss of data (due to unauthorized access) or malicious manipulation of business process sequences or activities. The task of risk management is to identify and treat the most critical risks without wasting resources for less severe problems. Within this paper, only the risk assessment part of the risk management process is addressed. More precisely, this paper reports the experiences made during the risk assessment for an industrial large scale software system Command Central.

© Springer International Publishing Switzerland 2015
F. Seehusen et al. (Eds.): RISK 2015, LNCS 9488, pp. 3–17, 2015.
DOI: 10.1007/978-3-319-26416-5_1

Risk assessment can be difficult and expensive. It typically depends on the skills and estimates of experts and manual risk assessment can only be performed at a high level of abstraction for large scale systems. Security testing is one risk analysis method that eventually yields objective results. But security testing itself might be hard and expensive, too. Manual testing is itself error prone and again infeasible for large scale systems. Choosing what should be tested and interpreting security test results are not trivial tasks. Indeed, even highly insecure systems can produce lots of correct test verdicts if the "wrong" test cases have been created and executed. Therefore, it makes sense to do Risk Assessment COMbined with Automated Testing, i.e. to use the RACOMAT method and the RACOMAT tool introduced here. RACOMAT has been developed along the case study in order to deal exactly with the challenges of large scale networked systems. Both, the development of RACOMAT and the risk assessment of Command Central are still ongoing.

1.1   The Case Study

The software under analysis is called Command Central [14] from Software AG, a tool from the webMethods tool suite allowing release managers, infrastructure engineers, system administrators, and operators to perform administrative tasks from a single location. Command Central assist the configuration, management, and monitoring by supporting the following tasks:

- Infrastructure engineers can see at a glance which products and fixes are installed, where they are installed, and compare installations to find discrepancies.
- System administrators can configure environments by using a single web user interface or command-line tool. Maintenance involves minimum effort and risk.
- Release managers can prepare and deploy changes to multiple servers using command-line scripting for simpler, safer lifecycle management.
- Operators can monitor server status and health, as well as start and stop servers from a single location. They can also configure alerts to be sent to them in case of unplanned outages.

Command Central is built on top of Software AG Common Platform, which uses the OSGi (Open Services Gateway Initiative) framework. Product-specific features are in the form of plug-ins.

Command Central users can communicate with Command Central Server using either the graphical web user interface for administering products using the web, or the Command line interface for automating administrative operations. An architecture overview of the Command Central software is provided in Fig. 1.

The Command Central Server accepts administrative commands that users submit through one of the user interfaces and directs the commands to the respective Platform Manager for subsequent execution. An installation in Command Central means one or more instances of the products that Command Central can manage. It provides a common location for configuring managed products installed in different environments.

The webMethods Platform Manager manages other Software AG products. Platform Manager enables Command Central to centrally administer the lifecycle of

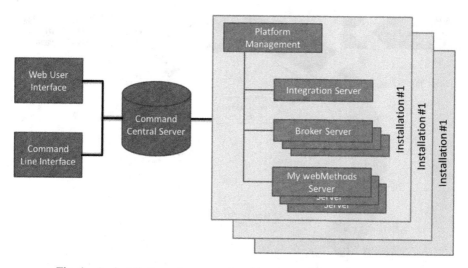

Fig. 1. An installation set-up scenario with command central management

managed products. In a host machine, there might be multiple Software AG product installations. For each Software AG product installation, a separate Platform Manager is needed to manage the installed products.

2   State of the Art

Security critical ICT systems should be carefully managed especially with respect to the related security risks. Such a risk management should include well-known concepts like risk assessment (ISO 31000 – [2]) and security testing (ISO 29119 – [3]).

2.1   Risk Assessment

According to the ISO 31000 standard, risk assessment means to identify, analyze and evaluate risks which could damage or destroy assets [2]. Lots of different methods and technologies for risk assessment have evolved, including fault tree analysis (FTA) [5], event tree analysis ETA [6], Failure Mode Effect (and Criticality) Analysis FMEA/FMECA [4] and the CORAS method [1].

Compositional risk assessment allows analysts to deal with manageable small components of a complex large scale modular system. It combines the individual risk assessment results for components to derive a risk picture for the entire complex system without looking further into the details of its components. However, most traditional risk assessment technologies analyze systems as a whole [7]. They do not offer support for compositional risk assessment. Nevertheless there are some publications dealing with compositional risk assessment and suggesting extensions for the mentioned risk assessment concepts, e.g. [8] for FTA and [9] for FMEA or [10] for CORAS, which is used in the case study presented here.

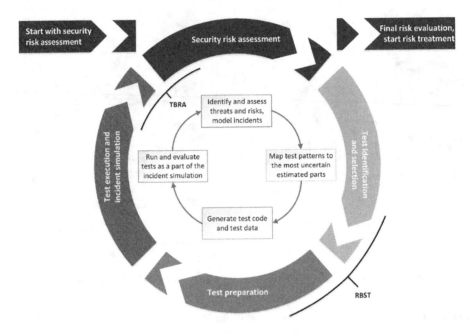

Fig. 2. The RACOMAT method

There are huge databases of common weaknesses, attack patterns and safeguards available that can be used as a base for security risk assessment, for example Mitre CWE [23] and CAPEC [22] or BSI IT-Grundschutz [21]. There are also vulnerability databases that list specific vulnerabilities for existing software programs, e.g. Mitre CVE [24]. Such information could be helpful in compositional risk assessment for systems that use listed programs or that have them in their environment. The mentioned catalogues are used in the case study introduced here.

2.2 Security Testing and Testing Combined with Risk Assessment

The ISO 29119 standard defines security testing as a type of testing that tries to evaluate the protection level of the system under test against unauthorized access, unwanted use and denial of service [3].

Traditional testing is a method to analyze the behavior of a system according to its specified functionality and expected results. Security testing in contrast also tests for unspecified behavior and for unexpected results. Hence, compared to other types of testing, for security testing it is harder to decide what should actually be tested and is more challenging to interpret the observed behavior.

One possible way to deal with the challenges of security testing is to combine it with risk assessment. ISO 29119 defines risk-based testing as a general method that uses risk assessment results to guide and to improve the testing process [3]. Risk analysis results can be used to define test policies and strategies, to identify what should actually be tested and how much effort should be spend for it. For instance, Kloos et al.

use fault trees for identifying test cases [15]. Stallbaum and Metzger automated the generation and prioritization of test cases based upon risk assessment artefacts [16]. Even (semi-) automated risk-based security testing might be expensive. Reusing testing artefacts for recurring security testing problems might help to reduce the effort. Security test patterns have been suggested for that purpose [17], but currently there is no extensive library of useful security test patterns available.

Risk assessment and testing can also interact the other way around: in test-based risk assessment, test results are used to identify, analyze and evaluate risks. There are several publications about this approach [18, 19], but there is still no general applicable method and not much tool support.

The concepts of risk-based testing and test-based risk assessment can also be combined. While Erdogan et al. propose such a combination [18], they do not propose any technique or detailed guideline for how to update the risk model based on the test results. The combined method with tool support presented in [20] has been developed further along the case study presented here and it was named the RACOMAT method and tool.

2.3   Simulation

Simulations that work with simplifying models in general can be very helpful to analyze large scale systems. For instance, Monte Carlo simulations can be used to analyze the behavior of complex systems and especially for calculating likelihood values in the risk aggregation process [11, 12].

In [13] it is described how Monte Carlo simulations and security testing can be used together within an iterative risk assessment process in order to refine the risk picture. This approach is used in the case study described here.

3   Requirements, Problems and Expectations

Large scale networked computer systems and software programs can be enormous complex. Building and maintaining such systems is challenging and it can be very expensive. One way to reduce costs without reducing the product features and the product quality is to let as much work as possible be done automatically by machines.

However, in the production and lifecycle management process for software there is usually only limited potential for automation. It typically requires lots of creative work which nowadays has to be done manually, e.g. modelling or writing code directly.

Nevertheless, at least for analytical and recurring tasks in the software development and maintenance process, a high level of automation should be achievable.

These promising candidates for automation include especially testing as a vital part of the software quality management. Indeed, within a testing process, many tasks can be automated, especially test data generation and test case execution. There are lots of tools supporting automated testing. Testing for specified behavior can be more or less completely automated if the specification is well modeled – test cases can be derived automatically from such a model. Of course, appropriate models have to be created manually in the first place. Additionally, interpreting the test results and reacting properly on them will always require further manual work.

For security testing, automation is probably slightly more difficult than for other types of testing like functional testing or integration testing. Security testing requires to test for unspecified behavior, so there is obviously no trivial way to derive all relevant test cases from a specification. Deciding what might be security critical and what should therefore be tested is a very difficult task because complete testing is infeasible for complex systems. Once having decided what should be tested, with testing techniques like fuzzing, it might be possible to automatically generate great many security relevant test cases. But that is only the easier part of security testing. Judging automatically whether a test has passed or failed can be quit challenging. For security tests it is often not at all clear what behavior could be triggered. Observing and interpreting unexpected incidents is indeed tricky. There is no point in generating automatically lots of test cases if all test results could be false positives or false negatives: the required further investigations would probably lead to an amount of manual work, which would be higher than simply doing manual testing with fewer, but eventually better designed test cases.

In contrast to testing, risk assessment is typically done with lots of manual effort. Conventional risk identification and risk analysis heavily depend on expert work and expert judgement. There are tools for risk assessment, but still questioners have to be answered, risk models have to be created and managed – so there is still a lot of work that has to be done more or less manually. Hence, for complex large scale systems, traditional risk assessment can only be performed at a high abstraction level.

We believe that the combination of risk assessment and security testing will lead to a better level of automatization for both concepts. Incident simulations are a third analytical concept that could be used to integrate them into a single process.

Besides automation, component based techniques are another important approach to deal with complexity. Compositional risk Assessment allows to treat small manageable components more or less independent from each other. Results for individual components are composed to a big picture without looking again in the details of the components. This is especially helpful for continuous risk assessment of systems that are gradually updated because it limits the need to reassess the risk to those components that have actually changed.

To be able to conduct efficient risk assessment of newly implemented features is a very appealing feature in software industries. Whenever a new feature is addressed by development, the assessment should be updated in order to make sure it contains a careful analysis of the new or altered product. Risk assessment must continuously assure that the risks are not only identified at lowest component level, but also for the higher component levels and single product levels up to the product suite level. Traces between the same risk artifacts at different abstraction levels should be tracked and preserved.

Risk evaluation should be possible at any level of abstraction. If for example some likelihood value for a risk was determined with the help of security testing, then it should be possible to look into the details of individual test cases and test results. But it should also be possible to view just the top level risks for all the program suites in which the tested component is used. A tool for risk assessment and security testing should support such transparent views. Additionally, it should provide at any level of abstraction information what the individual technical risk artefacts mean for the organizational management, e.g. how they affect business processes and what legal consequences unwanted incidents might have. Aggregated risk assessment results and risk pictures with connections to their non-technical impacts are suitable as a basis for decision making.

At the beginning of the research work for the presented case study, there was no risk assessment tool available that fulfills these expectations of interdisciplinary transparency and seamless integration with security testing.

Software products are implemented according to an intended environment and intended usage scenarios. Risk sensitivity in different environments and scenarios can vary in the sense that the product may be suitable for a particular setting (for which it was initially designed) but exhibits an unacceptable risk which prohibits the use in another, even more critical setting. In our view security should not be seen as a goal in itself, but a means of protecting assets. Cyber security must be understood and reasoned about not just at a technical level, but also at a non-technical level, taking into account the context in which software is used, organizational level assets, and legal issues. The producers of software systems cannot do the complete risk assessment for all potential customers because they do not have insight in the various contexts in which their products may be used. Therefore, software products should be provided with reusable risk assessment artefacts so that the risk of using them in a certain context can be evaluated by the potential customers and users themselves.

4 An Integrated Risk Assessment and Security Testing Approach

4.1 Initial Risk Assessment

The work on the case study started according to the ISO 31000 standard with establishing the context and risk identification phases. During these initial phases the product under investigation has been modelled in the ARIS RASEN framework. This has been achieved in a joint workshop with a software engineer as a representative from the product development (Command Central Product Development), a security expert overviewing and ensuring the compliance to security standards, and the RASEN project development team in charge of the implementation. As a result of the workshop the software under consideration has been modelled and weaknesses and risks from the CWE database have been assigned to the product and its components.

These first steps were done manually with the help of an existing risk artefact database. Hence, the initial assessment took place at a high level of abstraction in order to keep the manual effort reasonable low. Nevertheless, lots of information has been collected: for some of the about 30 components up to 27 different potential vulnerabilities have been identified – no less than 11 weaknesses for any component. This initial phase did neither analyze if the weaknesses actually exist nor how likely it is that the existing ones would actually be exploited. Its result is also not detailed enough to be very helpful as a starting point for risk-based security testing. Obviously, further analysis was required.

4.2   Refining the Risk Picture

For a more detailed risk analysis in which automated security testing can be used to get reliable objective results, the RACOMAT method and the RACOMAT tool have been developed. The core of the RACOMAT method is the iterative RACOMAT process (shown in Fig. 1) combines risk assessment and automated security testing in both ways: Test-Based Risk Assessment (TBRA), which tries to improve risk assessment with the results of security tests and Risk-Based Security Testing (RBST), which tries to optimize security testing with results of risk assessment. The method itself is basically following the concepts described in [20].

The development made along the Command Central case study was basically to improve the applicability for large scale networked systems.

The first idea that came to mind in order to reduce the manual effort of low level risk assessment was to integrate techniques for automated static analysis of components into the RACOMAT tool. Given (X)HTML pages, source program code, compiled libraries or programs, the RACOMAT static analysis tries to identify the public interfaces of any components and especially the functions as well as ports that could be used for interaction with other components or users. Thereby initial system models can be generated without requiring manual actions. The generated threat interfaces contain signatures with input and output ports, which can be associated with risk artefacts. Threat interfaces are low level enough to be used for automated testing, for example.

While the static analysis works fine for some software systems, especially for small exemplary programs, it does not in general produce good results. For Command Central, the current state of the RACOMT tool static analysis proved not to be very helpful. This was a kind of surprising because the main graphical Command Central user interface is a web based user interface and the RACOMAT tool is in general capable to statically analyze HTML user interfaces. However, the way Command Central builds HTML pages containing not much more than lots of script function calls, identifying interface elements is already difficult. Additionally, the user interfaces are generated dynamically based on the session state.

To enable the RACOMAT tool to deal with Command Central and other software systems with highly state dependent interfaces, it has been extended with dynamical analysis features. The dynamical analysis records information while the system is actually used. For the recording process it does not really matter if the system is used by human beings manually or if it is controlled by tools with automated test cases that are executed and monitored. Recording can especially also take place while the RACOMAT tool itself executes security tests.

Technically, the recording can take place at different levels. For a web based application like Command Central, it is probably a good idea to record messages at the Hypertext Transfer Protocol layer. Therefore, a little proxy server has been developed and integrated into the RACOMAT tool. This proxy server can be used to monitor and to manipulate the communication between Web Clients and Web Servers.

The recorded information can be used to generate interface descriptions automatically. For example, the RACOMAT tool can extract the target name and the parameter names from a HTTP PUT request. Based on this data, it can generate a meaningful

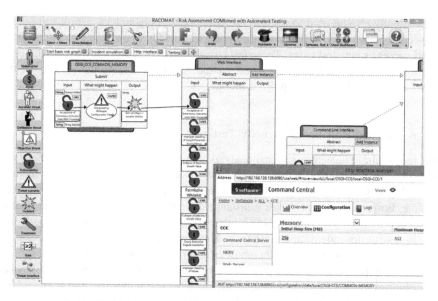

Fig. 3. The RACOMAT assistant for analyzing HTTP dynamically

signature for the entire specific request with ports for input and output, which can be added as a part of some threat interface to the risk model (Fig. 3).

A complete threat interface represents a component of the system, eventually in a specific state, and the immediately related risk analysis artefacts (i.e. weaknesses, attack patterns, faults …). In the case study presented here, there were already initial risk assessment artefacts which are imported from the ARIS tool into the RACOMAT tool. This includes a list of potential vulnerabilities for the entire web interface component, which is represented as an abstract threat interface in the RACOMAT risk model after the import. From the dynamic analysis, the RACOMAT tool generates more detailed threat interface descriptions for specific states. These state dependent threat interfaces can be linked with the more abstract threat interface for the entire Command Control web interface. The analysts can quickly go to through the list of potential vulnerabilities identified for the abstract threat interface and decide which of the vulnerabilities might exist for the more detailed state dependent threat interfaces and add those to the state dependent threat interfaces. This is basically like using a check list.

Furthermore, different state dependent threat interfaces can be linked with each other so that the sequence of how the states were reached is represented correctly in the risk model.

In addition to recording information about the signature of requests, the RACO-MAT tool can of course also extract the value for each parameter in a request. This information can eventually be used to decide about what type of information might be expected, e.g. an ASCII string or an integer. This might already indicate which potential weaknesses should be investigated most carefully.

Even more important, the values themselves might become vital for any following security test case generation and test execution. First, the recorded values can be used again in order to reach another state in a sequence of states. Second, the same values can eventually also be used to test for vulnerability to reply attacks. Third, valid input values can be used very well as a starting point for fuzzing in order to generate slightly altered values as new test cases. These test cases altered values that are eventually only close to valid input values are good test candidates for analyzing the security of the system under test against manipulated input.

4.3   Automated Risk-based Security Testing

After the semi-automated dynamical analysis, the risk model is much more detailed, but it still does not contain enough information to start security testing without manual effort. The RACOMAT tool provides assistants that can add more information from literature. For example, the CAPEC assistant can be used to add all the relevant related attack patterns from the Mitre CAPEC database for each identified potential vulnerability in a state dependent threat interface. Thereby, the attack patterns can be immediately linked with the related vulnerabilities and threat interface ports.

The attack patterns can be seen as security testing instructions. However, they do not contain executable test cases or machine readable test templates. The RACOMAT tool does provide an extendable library of predefined security test patterns which can be used to generate and execute test cases automatically once the pattern is instantiated. If no appropriate test patterns exist in the library, the tool allows its users to create new test patterns within the tool and to upload them to the library for sharing. Security test patterns are automatically associated with the attack patterns that can be tested using them. For instantiation, all that has to be done is assigning the potential observable results (i.e. unwanted incidents) to some output ports of the threat interfaces.

Based on likelihood and consequence estimates in the risk model, the RACOMAT tool can calculate the priority of the test patterns in order to spend the testing budget for the most critical tests. Likelihood estimates need only be made for base incidents. The RACOMAT tool can calculate likelihood values for dependent incidents by doing Monte Carlo simulations over the risk model. Of course, this requires that the relations between incidents are modeled accurately. Using the RACOMAT tool, dependencies between faults or incidents can be modeled in detail using directed weighted relations and gates. This might require some manual work. Without creating an accurate model, simulations or other calculations for dependent likelihood values are impossible.

Given an appropriately instantiated test pattern, test generation, test execution and test result aggregation are at least semi-automated. But for example for overflow tests, even complete automation is achievable using the RACOMAT tool. The entire security testing process is controlled from the risk assessment perspective, there is no gap in the workflow.

4.4   Test-based Risk Assessment

Testing results can be used to identify new unwanted incidents that have not been considered in the risk model so far. The RACOMAT tool is capable of adding such unexpected incidents semi-automatically to the risk graphs.

Furthermore, test results should be used to create a model that approximates the behavior of the tested parts accurately so that this model can be used in future incidents simulations which are used to calculate dependent likelihood values. Security testing in RACOMAT tool means trying to trigger unwanted incidents. The model that has to be crated should tell how likely it is that the tested incident will ever be triggered. So a likelihood expression should be interpolated from the raw test results. Likelihood expressions for Incidents are exactly the base for the RACOMAT tool incident simulations.

But how can a likelihood expression be interpolated from testing results if testing was not nearby complete? Since sound interpretation is highly dependent on the tests themselves, security testing metrics which contain interpolation functions can be chosen from the RACOMAT tool predefined suggestions or created and applied manually. Test patterns should indicate which predefined security test metrics are most appropriate to analyze the testing process and the test results. Any function of a security testing metric will expect information about the executed test cases and about the results that are observed with the help of the observation strategies of the test pattern. Some metric's functions might need further information, for example about the test execution time or about the entire time spend on testing including the instantiation of the test pattern. Security test patterns contain information that helps assigning the input parameters of the suggested metrics and calling the metric functions correctly. This bridging between a test pattern and a suggested testing metric can work automatically or at least semi-automatically.

Hence, it is possible to update the risk graphs automatically with more precise likelihood estimates interpolated from test results or with new faults based on unexpected test results.

After each iteration in the iterative RACOMAT process (i.e. after each security testing of some attack pattern), an incident simulation should be made to calculate updated likelihood values for dependent incidents before the most pressures threat scenarios which should be tested next are selected by the RACOMAT tool test prioritization algorithm.

4.5   Reusability, Configurations and High Level Composition

Reusable risk artefacts are one important result of the RACOMAT risk assessment process. Typically lots of security testing will be done for individual components. The risk models created for the components can be reused wherever the component is used. After modeling dependencies between the models of the components, the individual components do not have to be analyzed and tested again. The RACOMAT tool is capable of calculating likelihood values and risk values for any configuration that is modeled with the help of incident simulations.

Within the RACOMAT tool, the risk models used for incident simulations are directed weighted graphs with gates, somehow like fault trees. However, in RACOMAT, graphs are not required to be trees – nor to be acyclic at all. This allows to model mutual dependencies and things like build in repairing features easily, but it also makes simulations more challenging. To enable deterministic incident simulations in cyclic graphs, the RACOMAT tool requires users to break the loop at some point for single rounds in the simulation.

4.6   Continuing Risk Management

Creating a more detailed, more complete risk model with more precise values and being able to assess any composition in any context is not the final goal of a risk assessment process. While refining is a necessary step and while with the level of automation the RACOMAT tool offers this step is manageable, it also has some drawbacks. Especially, it makes the risk model way more complex. The managers do eventually not want to see all the details all the time. A good condensed overview is much better fitting their needs, especially if they can go into the details of the analysis if they decide to take a closer look. Therefore, after going into most detailed low level risk assessment, it is necessary to make sure that more abstract, higher level results are produced, too, and that these are linked with the low level results appropriately.

For example, for Command Central, finally only the risk artefacts identified for the entire abstract web interface are regarded to be of interest for the management. The risk values for the abstract high level threat interface of the web interface are updated based on the security test results for the many state dependent threat interfaces. The RACOMAT tool automatically calculates these updates with its incident simulations. Additionally, it provides high level dashboard views to support the further risk management.

Currently experiments are going on trying to allow for even higher abstraction using grouping and tagging for the risks based on information from literature und existing catalogues. First results seem promising especially for the tagging because it offers more flexibility.

In general the RACOMAT tool can be used as a stand-alone tool. It covers the entire process of combined test-based risk assessment (TBRA) and risk-based security testing (RBST) shown in Fig. 2. Nevertheless, it is also possible to use other possibly more specialized tools for some steps in that process. In the Case study presented here, the results of the risk assessment are integrated back into the models used by the ARIS

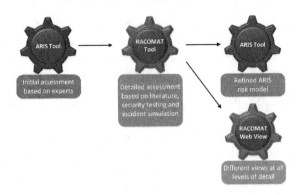

Fig. 4. The different tools used within the case study

framework tools. ARIS is established and widely used by the security experts and the developers responsible for Command Central. Therefore, the RACOMAT tool exports results in a JSON format that ARIS tools can import. However, the some results cannot be imported into ARIS models. In order to make them accessible even for managers and developers who do not want to use the RACOMAT tool, the development of a RACOMAT server has started that provides views with different levels of detail through a web interface (Fig. 4).

5   Conclusion and Future Work

The shown case study has lead massive extensions of the RACOMAT tool. Manly not to make the risk assessment theoretically more accurate, but to increase the level of automation and the usability was the major concern. With appropriate security test patterns and security testing metrics, it is possible to do a more or less completely automated Risk-Based Security Testing and Test-Based Security Risk Assessment with the RACOMAT tool.

The biggest problem at the moment is that there are only a few security testing metrics defined. The same is also true for the security test patterns – for many threat scenarios an attack patterns, there are currently no existing appropriate security test patterns. As long as these have to be created manually for each new attack pattern, the effort is just as high as for manual security testing. However, if there is a good pattern with sound metrics, then it can be instantiated for all occurrences of the same threat scenario with low manual configuration effort. Once there are extensive catalogues of patterns and metrics, then the concepts presented here will make the entire combined risk assessment and security testing process much easier and really safe a lot of manual work.

Creating a library of good security test patterns and security testing metrics is not a trivial task. With the RACOMAT tool, there is now at least a tool that supports creating and editing testing metrics as well as test patterns. This allows users to create the metrics and patterns needed.

Currently, a RACOMAT server for sharing test patterns, testing metrics and also for sharing reusable threat interfaces for entire components or programs is being developed. Sharing threat interfaces will be essential for allowing customers to do risk assessments for their specific environments, configurations and requirements themselves. For the future, the hope is that an open community will work with the threat interface, test pattern and testing metrics databases, developing them further in collaboration. Expecting that user feedback will be essential for quality assurance and for continuous improvement, user feedback will be taken serious and hopefully it will become a vital part of the open risk artefact, test pattern and testing metric databases.

References

1. Lund, M.S., Solhaug, B., Stølen, K.: Model-Driven Risk Analysis – The CORAS Approach. Springer, Heidelberg (2011)
2. International Standards Organization. ISO 31000:2009(E), Risk management – Principles and guidelines, (2009)

3. International Standards Organization. ISO 29119 Software and system engineering - Software Testing-Part 1–4 (2012)
4. Bouti, A., Kadi, D.A.: A state-of-the-art review of FMEA/FMECA. Int. J. Reliab. Qual. Saf. Eng. **1**, 515–543 (1994)
5. International Electrotechnical Commission: IEC 61025 Fault Tree Analysis (FTA) (1990)
6. International Electrotechnical Commission: IEC 60300-3-9 Dependability management – Part 3: Application guide – Section 9: Risk analysis of technological systems – Event Tree Analysis (ETA) (1995)
7. Lund, M.S., Solhaug, B., Stølen, K.: Evolution in relation to risk and trust management. IEEE Comput. **43**(5), 49–55 (2010)
8. Kaiser, B., Liggesmeyer, P., Mäckel, O.: A new component concept for fault trees. In: 8th Australian Workshop on Safety Critical Systems and Software (SCS 2003), pp. 37–46. Australian Computer Society (2003)
9. Papadoupoulos, Y., McDermid, J., Sasse, R., Heiner, G.: Analysis and synthesis of the behaviour of complex programmable electronic systems in conditions of failure. Reliab. Eng. Syst. Saf. **71**(3), 229–247 (2001). Elsevier
10. Viehmann, J.: Reusing risk analysis results - an extension for the CORAS risk analysis method. In: 4th International Conference on Information Privacy, Security, Risk and Trust (PASSAT 2012), pp. 742–751. IEEE (2012). doi:10.1109/SocialCom-PASSAT.2012.91
11. Gleißner, W., Berger, T.: Auf nach Monte Carlo: Simulationsverfahren zur Risiko-Aggregation. RiskNews **1**, 30–37 (2004). doi:10.1002/risk.200490005. Wiley
12. Greenland, S.: Sensitivity analysis, monte carlo risk analysis, and bayesian uncertainty assessment. Risk Anal. **21**, 579–584 (2001)
13. Viehmann, J.: Towards integration of compositional risk analysis using Monte Carlo simulation and security Testing. In: Bauer, T., Großmann, J., Seehusen, F., Stølen, K., Wendland, M.-F. (eds.) RISK 2013. LNCS, vol. 8418, pp. 109–119. Springer, Heidelberg (2014)
14. Handbook: webMethods Command Central Help, Version 9.6, Software AG Darmstadt Germany, April 2014. http://documentation.softwareag.com/webmethods/wmsuites/wmsuite9-6/Command_Central_and_Platform_Manager/9-6_Command_Central_Help.pdf
15. Kloos, J., Hussain, T., and Eschbach, R.: Risk-based testing of safety-critical embedded systems driven by fault tree analysis. In: Software Testing, Verication and Validation Work-shops (ICSTW 2011), pp. 26–33. IEEE (2011)
16. Stallbaum, H., Metzger, A., Pohl, K.: An automated technique for risk-based test case generation and prioritization. In: Proceedings of Workshop on Automation of Software Test, AST 2008, Germany, pp. 67–70 (2008)
17. Smith, B.: Security Test Patterns (2008). http://www.securitytestpatterns.org/doku.php
18. Erdogan, G., Seehusen, F., Stølen, K., Aagedal, J.: Assessing the usefulness of testing for validating the correctness of security risk models based on an industrial case study. In: Proceedings of the Workshop on Quantitative Aspects in Security Assurance (QASA 2012), Pisa (2012)
19. Benet, A.F.: A risk driven approach to testing medical device software. In: Advances in Systems Safety, pp. 157–168. Springer (2011)
20. Großmann, J., Schneider, M., Viehmann, J., Wendland, M.-F.: Combining risk analysis and security testing. In: Margaria, T., Steffen, B. (eds.) ISoLA 2014, Part II. LNCS, vol. 8803, pp. 322–336. Springer, Heidelberg (2014)
21. Federal Office for Information Security (BSI): IT-Grundschutz Catalogues, Bonn Germany (2013). https://www.bsi.bund.de/EN/Topics/ITGrundschutz/ITGrundschutzCatalogues/itgrundschutzcatalogues_node.html

22. MITRE: Common Attack Pattern Enumeration and Classification, MITRE (2015). http://capec.mitre.org/
23. MITRE: Common Weakness Enumeration, MITRE (2015). http://cwe.mitre.org/data/index.html
24. MITRE: Common Vulnerabilities and Exposures, MITRE (2015). https://cve.mitre.org/cve/cve.html

Combining Security Risk Assessment and Security Testing Based on Standards

Jürgen Großmann[1(✉)] and Fredrik Seehusen[2]

[1] Fraunhofer FOKUS, Berlin, Germany
juergen.grossmann@fokus.fraunhofer.de
[2] SINTEF ICT, Oslo, Norway
fredrik.seehusen@sintef.no

Abstract. Managing cyber security has become increasingly important due to the growing interconnectivity of computerized systems and their use in society. A comprehensive assessment of cyber security can be challenging as its spans across different domains of knowledge and expertise. For instance, identifying cyber security vulnerabilities requires detailed technical expertise and knowledge, while the assessment of organizational impact and legal implications of cyber security incidents may require expertise and knowledge related to risk and compliance. Standards like ISO 31000 and ISO/IEC/IEEE 29119 detail the relevant aspects of risk management and testing and thus provide guidance in these areas. However, both standards are not exclusively dedicated to the subject of security and do not cover the explicit integration between security risk assessment and security testing. We think however, that they provide a good basis for that. In this paper we show how ISO 31000 and ISO/IEC/IEEE 29119 can be integrated to provide a comprehensive approach to cyber security that covers both security risk assessment and security testing.

1 Introduction

Security risk assessment and security testing both contribute to an overall assessment of the security of a system on different levels. Security risk assessment is the iterative process that analyses the potential threats to a system in order to calculate the likelihood of their occurrence and their consequence. It comprises the identification of assets, threats and vulnerabilities as well as the identification, specification and realisation of risk treatments. Security testing is dedicated to dynamically check the security properties of software. We generally distinguish functional security testing, robustness testing, performance testing and penetration testing. While security testing addresses technical security issues in particular, security risk assessment typically addresses higher level, non-technical issues as well. However, we believe that the systematic integration of activities that cover aspect from security testing, and security risk assessment provide added value to the overall goal in assessing the security of large scale, networked system. While the high level perspective of the security risk assessment can provide guidance (i.e. by helping focus on the relevant aspects) to the activities carried out during security testing, testing can provide factual feedback on the actual quality characteristics of a system and thus allow for improving the overall

© Springer International Publishing Switzerland 2015
F. Seehusen et al. (Eds.): RISK 2015, LNCS 9488, pp. 18–33, 2015.
DOI: 10.1007/978-3-319-26416-5_2

assessment of the system. Integrating and interweaving the activities from both sides allows for a more precise, focused and dynamic assessment of systems, processes and other targets.

We refer to the use of security testing to improve the security risk assessment process as test-based security risk assessment, and the use of security risk assessment to improve the security testing as risk-based security testing. In this paper, we will address both kinds of integration.

Security risk assessment and testing are both covered by existing standards such as ISO 31000 [8] and ISO/IEC/IEEE 29119 (referred to as ISO 29119 in the following) [9]. However, both standards are not explicitly dedicated to the subject of security and currently no standard exists that sufficiently emphasizes the systematic integration of security risk assessment and security testing. ISO 29119 is not directly dedicated to security testing and, even if ISO 29119 already describes interaction between testing and risk assessment, both standards do not cover a concise integration between security risk assessment and security testing. While the industry demands integrative approaches that cope with security as a whole, both areas are normally treated as distinct areas that are isolated from one another. This paper describes the, from our experience, relevant points of integration between security risk assessment and security testing. The points of integration cover activities driven from security risk assessment as well as from security testing. They are documented along standardized process flows from ISO 31000 and ISO 29119 so that they are easy to integrate when these standards are in use.

This paper is structured as follows: Sect. 2 provides an overview on approaches to risk assessment and security testing, Sect. 3 describes our general idea of integration and the Sects. 4 and 5 document the actual points of integration by defining the notion of test-based risk assessment and risk-based security testing. Section 6 concludes the paper.

2 State of the Art

Security risk assessment and security testing are traditionally addressed as distinct domains with their own methods and processes. Arguably, the most well known processes within the two domains are ISO 31000 for risk assessment and ISO 29119 for testing. However, currently no standard exists that sufficiently emphasizes the systematic integration of security risk assessment and security testing. Neither are we aware of any work that attempts to integrate the ISO 31000 and the ISO processes.

Many specific approaches that combine testing and risk assessment have been proposed. See [1, 3] for a comprehensive survey of these approaches. As discussed by Erdogan et al. [3], most of these approaches that combine risk assessment and testing focus on specific aspects of the risk or testing process such as test case generation or risk estimation. This is in contrast to our approach that addresses the whole process.

The approaches that we are aware of that addresses the combination of risk assessment and testing at a more general level as we do, are [2, 4, 5, 6, 7, 12, 13]. However, our work differs from these approaches in that none of the approaches describe the relationship to well-established standards within the risk assessment and the testing domains.

There are general technical recommendations on security testing techniques [7, 10, 11] that propose the use of risk analysis results to guide security testing. In a similar manner ISO 29119 addresses the use of risk assessment results to improve testing. However, these recommendations are very general in nature and describe in this sense no real method for risk-based testing.

3   Integrating Security Risk Assessment and Security Testing

The overall process of a combined security assessment described in this paper has been developed in the RASEN research project[1] and evaluated within 3 case studies. The process is derived from ISO-31000 and extended to highlight the integration with security testing. It is defined independent from any application domain and independent from the level, target or depth of the security assessment. It could be applied to any kind of technical security assessment and testing processes. The overall process covers two different workstreams that each consist of a combination of typical security risk assessment activities that are defined in ISO 31000 and typical security testing activities that follow testing standards like ISO 29119.

1. A test-based security risk assessment workstream starts like a typical risk assessment workstream and use testing results to guide and improve the risk assessment. Security testing is used to provide feedback on actually existing vulnerabilities that have not been covered during risk assessment or allows risk values to be adjusted on basis of tangible measurements like test results. Security testing should provide a concise feedback whether the properties of the target under assessment have been really met by the risk assessment.
2. The risk-based security testing workstream starts like a typical testing workstream and uses risk assessment results to guide and focus the testing. Such a workstream starts with identifying the areas of risk within the target's business processes and building and prioritizing the testing program around these risks. In this setting risks help focusing the testing resources on the areas that are most likely to cause concern or supporting the selection of test techniques dedicated to already identified threat scenarios.

According to Fig. 1, both workstreams start with a preparatory phase called *Establishing the Context* that includes preparatory activities like *Understanding the Business and Regulatory Environment* as well as the *Requirements & Process Identification*. During the first phase the high-level security objectives are identified and documented and the overall process planning is done. Moreover, the figure shows additional support activities like *Communication & Consult* and *Monitoring and Review* that are meant to set up the management perspective, thus to continuously control, react, and improve all relevant information and results of the process. From a process point of view, these activities are meant to provide the contextual and management related framework. The individual activities covered in these phases might differ in detail dependent on whether

---

[1] www.rasen-project.eu.

the risk assessment or testing activities are the guiding activities. The main phase, namely the *Security Assessment* phase covers the integration between the risk assessment workstream and a security testing workstream. This phase is detailed more closely in the following two sections.

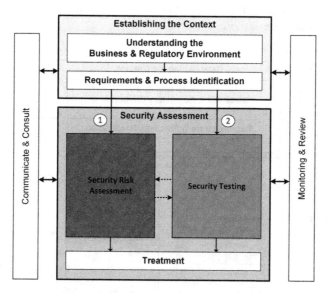

Fig. 1. The overall combined security assessment process

4   Test-Based Security Risk Assessment

Risk assessment is the overall process of risk identification, estimation, and evaluation. The typical outcome of a risk assessment is a set of treatments for unacceptable risks (if any) and a risk matrix that shows the risk values of identified risks. The information and knowledge on which a risk assessment is based has a big impact on the outcome of the risk assessment. The main reason for integrating testing into the risk assessment process is to use testing as a means of obtaining a better information basis on which to perform the risk assessment. Testing, as opposed to other forms of information gathering such as expert judgments and historical data, is particularly suited for obtaining low-level technical information which often is necessary for an accurate understanding of the target of evaluation.

From a testing perspective, the risk assessment can be used for representing test results in the context of risk assessment artefacts. This kind of high-level representation of test results can for instance be used to support management issues and control the overall test process during the test management.

In a test-based risk assessment, test results are used as explicit input to various activities of the risk assessment. Figure 2 shows how the overall security assessment process (shown in Fig. 1) is refined into a process for test-based risk assessment. Here the risk assessment activity has been decomposed into the three activities *Risk*

Identification, Risk Estimation, and *Risk Evaluation.* These three activities, together with the *Establishing the Context* and *Treatment* activities form the core of the ISO 31000 risk management process. As indicated in Fig. 2, there are in particular two places where testing can enhance the risk assessment process. The first, denoted 1 in the figure, is during risk identification, and the second is during risk estimation (denoted 2 in the figure). In the following, we describe in more detail how test results may be used as input to these activities.

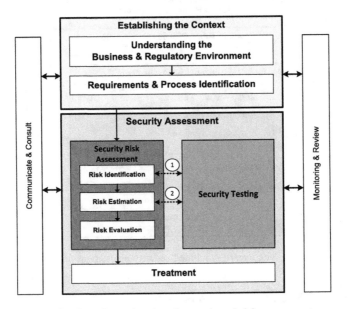

Fig. 2. Generic workstream for test-based risk assessment

4.1   Test-Based Risk Identification

Risk identification is the process of finding, recognizing and describing risks. This involves identifying sources of risk (e.g. threats and vulnerabilities), areas of impacts (e.g. the assets), events (including changes in circumstances), their causes and their potential consequences. The *Establishing the Context* activity is assumed to be performed before the risk identification. A typical starting point for the risk identification step is: a description of the target of evaluation, a definition of likelihood and consequence scales, risk evaluation criteria (often expressed in the form of risk matrices), and asset definitions.

The typical artefacts that are identified during the risk identification activity are threats, threat scenarios, vulnerabilities, and unwanted incidents that may constitute risks. In Fig. 3, we show how the risk identification can be structured w.r.t. to the identification of these artefacts. As indicated in the figure, there are in particular two activities that can be integrated with testing:

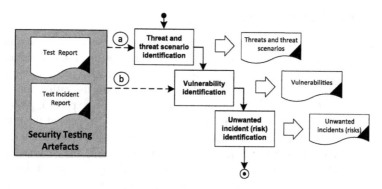

Fig. 3. Test-based risk identification

(a) Test-based threat and threat scenario identification
(b) Test-based vulnerability identification

In the following, we describe these activities in more detail.

4.1.1   Risk Identification: Test-Based Threat and Threat Scenario Identification (a)

The purpose of this activity is to identify threats and threat scenarios. A threat is a potential cause of an unwanted incident. A threat may be human or non-human, malicious or non-malicious. A hacker is an example of a typical malicious human threat. A threat scenario is a series of events that is initiated by a threat and that may lead to an unwanted incident. A cyber security attack such as SQL injection is a typical example of a threat scenario.

Testing can be used in order to obtain information that can support the identification of threats and threat scenarios. Particularly relevant in this setting are testing and analysis techniques that yield information about the interfaces/entry points, the attack-surface, and potential attacks against the target of evaluation. The tools that can be used for this purpose are typical security testing tools like network discovery tools, web-crawlers, and fuzz testing tools as well as analysis tools like static code analysis tools.

4.1.2   Risk Identification: Test-Based Vulnerability Identification (b)

A vulnerability is a weakness, flaw or deficiency that opens for, or may be exploited by, a threat to cause harm to or reduce the value of an asset. Test-based vulnerability identification refers to the use of testing to obtain information that supports the vulnerability identification activity. Testing techniques that yield information about the presence of actual vulnerabilities in the target of evaluation or *potential* vulnerabilities that *may* be present in the target of evaluation are relevant in this activity. The kinds of testing tools that can be used for this purpose are penetrating testing tools, model-based security testing tools, static and dynamic code analysis tools, and vulnerability scanners.

4.2   Test-Based Risk Estimation

Risk estimation is the process of estimating likelihood and consequences values for risks and their causes (i.e. threat scenarios). Accurate risk estimation is essential for a successful outcome of a risk assessment. However, risk estimation is one of the hardest activities of a risk assessment since the information basis for the estimation is often imprecise and insufficient, and we are often forced to rely on expert judgment. This might result in a high degree of uncertainty related to the correctness of the estimates.

As shown in Fig. 4, the risk estimation activity can be decomposed into the three sub-activities: Likelihood Estimation, Consequence Estimation, and Estimate Validation. The last sub-activity refers to checking and/or gaining confidence in the correctness of the risk estimates. As indicated in Fig. 4, there are in particular two activities that can be integrated with testing:

(a) Test-based likelihood estimation
(b) Test-based estimate validation

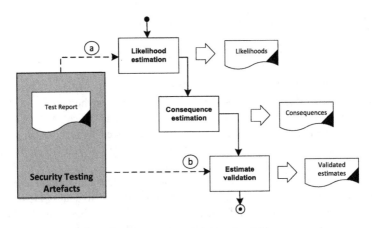

Fig. 4. Test-based risk estimation.

4.2.1   Risk Estimation: Test-Based Likelihood Estimation (a)

Likelihood estimation is the activity of estimating likelihoods for risks and their causes. In a security setting, this involves estimating the likelihood that: security attacks will be initiated; attacks will be successful if initiated; successful attacks will lead to identified risks. Likelihoods should be document using the likelihood scales defined in the *Establishing the Context* step of the risk assessment.

Testing is particularly relevant for obtaining information that can support the estimation of the likelihood that an attack will be successful if initiated. This is because security testing is most often used for identifying vulnerabilities, and the presence of these has a direct impact on this likelihood. Thus the testing techniques used for test-based likelihood estimation are similar to those used for test-based vulnerability identification (as described in Sect. 4.1.2). The main difference between these activities is that in the former, information about the vulnerabilities is only used as a means of supporting likelihood estimation.

4.2.2   Risk Estimation: Test-Based Estimate Validation (b)

Validation is the activity of checking or gaining confidence in the correctness of the estimated risk values. In a test-based setting, we recommend that uncertainty related to the correctness of an estimate be explicitly expressed. For instance, instead of using single likelihood values such as frequency or probability, we can use intervals of likelihoods to express the belief that the correct likelihood likes somewhere within the interval without knowing precisely where. Uncertainty can then be measured in terms of the breath of the interval - the broader the intervals, the more uncertainty there is.

As for the likelihood estimation activity, testing is particularly useful for obtaining information that supports the estimation of likelihood of successful attacks. The main difference between test-based likelihood estimation and test-based likelihood validation, is that in the former activity, testing is used to obtain the likelihood in the first place, whereas in the second activity, the purpose is to validate or gain confidence in the correctness of a likelihood value which as already been estimated. If uncertainty is expressed explicitly, the test results may be used lower this uncertainty value. For instance if likelihood intervals are used, the test results may result in a narrowing of the intervals. Recalculating the likelihood values of risks as a result of the updated uncertainty is a good way of showing how the test results have impacted the risks.

5   Risk-Based Security Testing

The risk-based security testing workstream is structured like a typical security testing process. It starts with a planning phase, a test design & implementation phase and ends with test execution, analysis and summary. The result of the risk assessment, i.e. the identified vulnerabilities, threat scenarios and unwanted incidents, are used to guide the test planning, test identification and may complement requirements engineering results with systematic information concerning the threats and vulnerabilities of a system.

Additional factors like probabilities and consequences can be additionally used to weight threat scenarios and thus help identifying which threat scenarios are more relevant and thus identifying the ones that need to be treated and tested more carefully. From a process point of view, the interaction between risk assessment and testing could be best described following the phases of a typical testing process. Figure 5 illustrates the three phases of a testing process that are affected and supported by risk-based security testing.

1. Risk-based security test planning deals with the integration of security risk assessment in the test planning process.
2. Risk-based security test design, implementation deals with the integration of security risk assessment in the test design and implementation process.
3. Risk-based test execution, analysis and summary deals with a risk-based test execution as well as with the systematic analysis and summary of test results.

5.1   Risk-Based Security Test Planning

According to ISO 29119, test planning is the activity of developing the test plan. It aims for determining the test objective, the test scope, and the risks associated to the

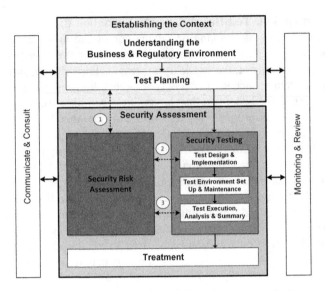

Fig. 5. Process model for risk-based security testing

overall testing process. The main outcome of test planning is a test strategy and a plan that depicts the staffing, the required resources, as well as a schedule for the individual testing activities. While functional testing is more or less guided directly by the system specification (i.e. features, requirements, architecture), security testing often is not. Security is a non-functional property and thus requires dedicated information that addresses the (security) context of the system. Security risk assessment can be used to roughly identify high-risk areas or features of the system under test (SUT) and thus determine and optimize the respective test effort. Moreover, a first assessment of the identified vulnerabilities and threat scenarios may help to select test strategies and techniques that are dedicated to deal with the most critical security risks. Figure 6 shows the integration of security risk assessment results in the overall test planning process. We have identified three integration activities that all serve different purposes:

(a) Integrate risk analysis
(b) Risk-based test strategy design
(c) Risk-based security resource planning and test scheduling

Before starting any of these activities, contextual information i.e. legal or regulatory requirements, organizational test and security policies, organizational or higher-level test strategies, and technical limitations as well as resource limitations and the security risk assessment results (threat, vulnerability and risk estimations) that capture the technical, business, regulatory, and legal requirements should be available.

5.1.1 Security Test Planning: Integrate Risk Analysis (a)

Typically, project risk analysis is a substantial part of the test planning process. The risk analysis is done to get an estimate on the specific project risks, considering the availability of test resources, considering specific product risks and other project related

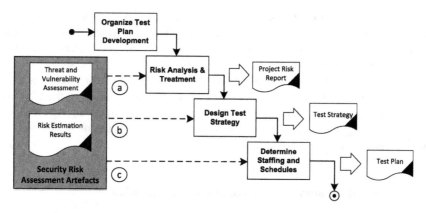

Fig. 6. Process model for risk-based security test planning

issues. The security risk assessment typically addresses the security risk of the product (i.e. the test item). As such, this kind of risk assessment can serve the project risk assessment with valuable estimates on the major product risks. The test manager should review the relevant security risks to identify those, which have a special role for security testing and should try to identify additional product and project related risks like missing resources, technical issues related to the test infrastructure etc. Finally, the test manager should develop an overall risk picture for the test project and communicate the risk picture to the Stakeholders.

5.1.2   Security Test Planning: Risk-Based Security Test Strategy Design (b)

A test strategy defines the test phases, the types of testing, the test techniques and the test completion criteria. A special challenge in security testing is the identification of dedicated and effective security testing techniques. This process could be optimized when the identification and selection of security testing techniques is based on the potential threats and vulnerabilities, which have been identified during a preceding security risk assessment. The test manager should assign vulnerabilities and threat scenarios to test items (interfaces, operations, components) and/or test conditions and try to identify the potential vulnerabilities that have the highest impact on the overall security risks when they are detected. Additionally, the test manager should assign test completion criteria to each test item and/or each test condition and prioritize test item and/or tor each test condition by considering the required test efforts to match the completion criteria and the impact testing may have on the overall security risks (i.e. when vulnerabilities are detected or test suites pass without detecting anything).

5.1.3   Security Test Planning: Risk-Based Security Resource Planning and Test Scheduling (c)

The second major activity during test planning is the identification and allocation of resources as well as the related schedule of all relevant security testing activities. Since the main task of security testing is finding vulnerabilities, resource planning and test schedules should be aligned with the major security risks so that resources and the order of testing allows for a focused testing of the test items or test condition where the detection of vulnerabilities shows the largest impact. The test manager should check for required security testing competences and should acquire new competences if certain security testing tasks require these competences. The test manager should allocate resources considering the required test efforts for that test items or test conditions where testing may have the largest impact in terms of treating or minimizing the identified security risks. He should plan the test schedules so that test items or test conditions where testing might have the largest impact in terms of treating or minimizing the identified security risks are tested first.

5.2   Risk-Based Security Test Design and Implementation

The test design and implementation process is mainly dedicated to derive the test cases and test procedures that are later on applied to the system under test. Security-risk assessment in general provides two different kinds of information that are useful within this process. On the one hand information on expected threats and potential vulnerabilities can be used to systematically determine and identify test conditions (testable aspects of a system) and test purposes. On the other hand side the security risk assessment provides quantitative estimations on the risks, i.e. the product of frequencies or probabilities and estimated consequences. This information can be used to select and prioritize either the test conditions or the actual tests when they are assembled to test sets. Risks as well as their probabilities and consequence values to set priorities for the test selection, test case generation as well as for the order of test execution expressed by risk-optimized test procedures.

Considering security testing, especially the derivation of test conditions and test coverage items are critical. A recourse to security risks, potential threat scenarios and potential vulnerabilities provide a good guidance which of the features and test conditions require testing, which coverage items should be covered in which depth and how individual test cases and test procedures should look like. Figure 7 shows the typical course of test design activities and the respective integration points with security risk assessment. Below, the associated and (through risk assessment) enhanced activities are listed.

(a) Risk-based identification and prioritization of features sets
(b) Risk-based derivation of test conditions and test coverage items
(c) Threat scenario based derivation of test cases
(d) Risk-based assembly of test procedures

5.2.1   Security Test Design: Risk-Based Identification and Prioritization of Features Sets (a)

A first step during the test design phase is the identification and categorization of the security features that will be tested. Since security features describe functional security measures this approach especially allows for testing the correctness of the feature implementation. Security risk assessment can be used to determine the most critical security features so that these features are tested more intensively and in more detail.

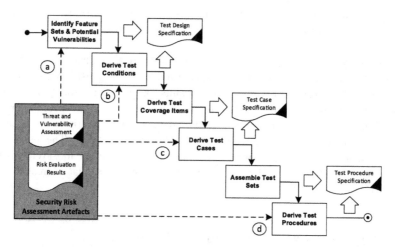

Fig. 7. Process model for risk-based security test design

The security tester should identify testable security features that need to be covered by security testing and prioritize them using the risk levels that are associated with the threat scenario/vulnerabilities.

5.2.2 Security Test Design: Risk-Based Derivation of Test Conditions and Test Coverage Items (b)

After a set of testable security features have been identified the security tester should derive the test conditions and test coverage items. This could be done on basis of the identified features (see phase a) but need to especially consider that security is a non-functional property and that a correct implementation of all security features may not ensure a secure system. Thus, additional test conditions and coverage items are required that especially address the detection of currently unknown vulnerabilities (vulnerability and robustness testing). Security risk assessment should be used to provide a systematic guidance for the derivation of especially these test conditions and test coverage items. Test coverage items and the respective test depth should be chosen according to the impact testing may have on the overall associated security risks.

5.2.3 Security Test Design: Threat Scenario Based Derivation of Test Cases (c)

In this step, the security tester should derive test cases on basis of test conditions and test coverage items. The security tester determines the pre-conditions for the individual tests by selecting adequate input values, the actions to exercise the selected test coverage items, and determines the expected results. Since security risk assessment has been used to identify the test conditions and the test coverage items it is already considered through the activities before. However, threat scenarios and potential vulnerabilities that have been identified during risk assessment might still help by identifying the preconditions, input values, actions and expected results in case it has not been done before. The test designer should identify the preconditions for the tests, the test data, the test actions and the expected results by examining the test conditions, test coverage items, threat scenarios and potential vulnerabilities.

5.2.4   Security Test Design: Risk-Based Assembly of Test Procedures (d)

In this step, the test cases should be assembled to test sets and test procedures. While test sets group test cases with common constraints on test environment or test items, test procedures defines the order of test execution and thus have to respect the pre- and post conditions. Security risk assessment should be used to prioritize the order test cases and thus the order of testing with respect to the associated risks. The test designer should assemble test sets and test procedures in such a way, that the most relevant tests are executed first. The most relevant test cases are the test cases that address the most critical risks.

5.3   Risk-Based Test Execution, Analysis and Summary

The decision of how extensive testing should be is always a question of the remaining test budget, the remaining time and the probability to discover even more critical errors, vulnerabilities or design flaws. Risk-based test execution allows the prioritization of already existing test cases, test sets or test procedure during regression testing. Risk-based security test analysis and summary aims for improving the evaluation of the test progress by introducing the notion of risk coverage and remaining risks on basis of the intermediate test results as well as on basis of the errors, vulnerabilities or flaws that have been found during testing. In summary we have identified the following three activities that are supported through results from security risk assessment (Fig. 8).

(a)   Risk-based test execution prioritization
(b)   Risk-based test analysis
(c)   Risk-based test summary

5.3.1   Test Execution, Analysis and Summary: Risked-Based Test Execution Prioritization (a)

The execution of test cases can be done several times for the same test cases and test procedures. Normally the execution order for test cases and test procedures is determined at test design by the assembly of test procedures. However, there are a number of regression test scenarios where reprioritization becomes necessary. In this case a risk-based approach for test executions prioritization may help to cover the most relevant remaining security risks. The security tester should prioritize test cases and test procedures in such a way that the most relevant tests are executed first. The most relevant test cases are the test cases that address the most critical risks.

5.3.2   Test Execution, Analysis and Summary: Risked-Based Test Analysis (b)

The test analysis process is used for the evaluation of the test results and the reporting of test incidents. This process will be entered after the test execution and it mainly covers the analysis and evaluation of test failures and issues where something unusual

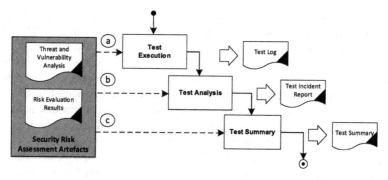

Fig. 8. Process model for risk-based test execution, analysis and summary

or unexpected occurred during test execution. Its main purpose is to categorize the issues that occurred during testing and put them into context so that the test manager can rate them. The security tester should classify newly identified incidents by means of their relation to artefacts from the security risk assessment (e.g., risks, threat scenarios, vulnerabilities) and prioritize the newly identified incidents by means of associated artefacts from the security risk assessment. Issues related to critical risks should be rated higher than the ones that are associated with minor risks. New and/or updated incidents are communicated to the relevant stakeholders.

5.3.3 Test Execution, Analysis and Summary: Risked-Based Test Summary (c)

Finally, the overall test results, i.e. the test verdicts, the issues and their categorization are summarized such that the stakeholder can understand the outcome of the tests. The security tester should analyse the test logs and separate security risks that have been tested successfully (all tests are passed) and those that have not been tested successfully (issues have been found). He should (re-) characterize the security risks by interpreting the test results and make use of dedicate test metrics to determine the quality of test procedures and thus the significance and validity of the test results.

6 Conclusion and Future Work

The integration of risk assessment and security testing offers a number of advantages that are intuitive and easy to grasp. In fact, a non-systematic integration of these two workstream has already been applied in practical settings. Integrating risk assessment artefacts in the security testing process allow for a concise selection of test techniques, the adequate choice of the required expertise and it supports the targeted prioritization of testing tasks and test cases. Additionally, the interpretation of the test results in the context of a security risk analysis can provide a meaningful feedback to the management level. In addition, security testing can be used to complement the assumptions made during risk assessment with a factual basis obtained by the tests.

The method for security assessment described in this paper provides a comprehensive approach to cyber security assessment and management. It might address low-level technical issues as well as high-level non-technical issues. The method integrates two areas that are traditionally addressed in isolation: security risk assessment and security testing. Each of the two areas is represented by an individual workstream, so that they could be processed independent from each other and at different points in time. The overall process of each of the workstreams is based on recognized standards, namely ISO 31000 and ISO 29119 and thus allow for an easy integration in industrial settings. In the past, we have been able to repeatedly elaborate useful integration scenarios based on the proposed integration scheme. The workstreams and their points of integration were successfully evaluated within several case studies representing relevant industrial domains like banking, e-Health and software development. In the near future, we will provide systematic guidance on how to apply our method to dedicated fields of application. We will provide tailored instantiation of our method to serve the special requirements coming from areas like cyber security, information security and critical infrastructure protection. Moreover we will show how our approach can be integrated in the different phases and with the different activities of a typical system life cycle.

Acknowledgements. This work has been conducted as a part of EU project RASEN (316853) funded by the European Commission within the 7th Framework Program.

References

1. Alam, M., Khan, A.I.: Risk-based testing techniques: a perspective study. Int. J. Comput. Appl. **65**, 33–41 (2013)
2. Amland, S.: Risk-based testing: Risk analysis fundamentals and metrics for software testing including a financial application case study. J. Syst. Softw. **53**(3), 287–295 (2000)
3. Erdogan, G., Li, Y., Runde, R., Seehusen, F., Stølen, K.: Approaches for the combined use of risk analysis and testing: A systematic literature review. Int. J. Softw. Tools Technol. Transfer **16**, 627–642 (2014)
4. Felderer, M., Haisjackl, C., Breu, R., Motz, J.: Integrating manual and automatic risk assessment for risk-based testing. In: Biffl, S., Winkler, D., Bergsmann, J. (eds.) SWQD 2012. LNBIP, vol. 94, pp. 159–180. Springer, Heidelberg (2012)
5. Felderer, M., Ramler, R.: Experiences and challenges of introducing risk-based testing in an industrial project. In: Winkler, D., Biffl, S., Bergsmann, J. (eds.) SWQD 2013. LNBIP, vol. 133, pp. 10–29. Springer, Heidelberg (2013)
6. Felderer, M., Schieferdecker, I.: A taxonomy of risk-based testing. Int. J. Softw. Tools Technol. Transfer **16**(5), 559–568 (2014)
7. Herzog, P.: OSSTMM 2.1. Open-Source Security Testing Methodology Manual; Institute for Security and Open Methodologies (2003)
8. International Standards Organization. ISO 31000:2009(E), Risk management – Principles and guidelines (2009)
9. International Standards Organization. ISO/IEC/IEEE 29119 Software and system engineering - Software Testing-Part 1-4 (2012)

10. Michael, C.C., Radosevich, W.: Risk-Based and Functional Security Testing. Cigital, Inc. (2005)
11. Murthy, K.K., Thakkar, K.R., Laxminarayan, S.: Leveraging risk based testing in enterprise systems security validation. In: Proceedings of the First Int Emerging Network Intelligence Conference, pp. 111–116 (2009)
12. Redmill, F.: Exploring risk-based testing and its implications: research articles. Softw. Test. Verif. Reliab. **14**(1), 3–15 (2004)
13. Redmill, F.: Theory and practice of risk-based testing: Research Articles. Softw. Test. Verif. Reliab. **15**(1), 3–20 (2005)

Validation of IT Risk Assessments with Markov Logic Networks

Janno von Stülpnagel$^{(\boxtimes)}$ and Willy Chen

Softplant GmbH, Agnes-Pockels-Bogen 1, 80992 Munich, Germany
{janno.stuelpnagel,willy.chen}@softplant.de
http://www.softplant.de/

Abstract. Risk assessments of big and complex IT infrastructures comprise numerous qualitative risk estimations for infrastructure assets. Qualitative risk estimations, however, are subjective and thus prone to errors. We present an approach to detect anomalies in the result of risk assessments by considering information about inter-dependencies between various building blocks of IT landscapes from enterprise architecture management. We therefore integrate data from enterprise architecture and risk estimations using Semantic Web technologies and formalize common anomalies such as inconsistent estimations of dependent infrastructure components. To reflect the uncertainty of qualitative analyses we utilize Markov logic networks (MLN) to validate the resulting model and determine more probable and consistent estimations.

Keywords: IT risk management · Markov logic networks · Risk assessment · Validation · Semantic web · OWL2-QL

1 Introduction

IT is a critical factor for modern enterprises. Therefore the business risks resulting from the usage of IT have to be managed in an appropriate manner. IT risk management is a systematic approach concerned with the identification of threats and vulnerabilities as well as the initiation of countermeasures for security risks. Risk assessment, a critical task within IT risk management, focuses on identifying threats for components in an IT infrastructure and estimating the risk level. These assessments are primarily based on qualitative expert opinions [1]. Despite the size and complexity of IT infrastructures - especially in large enterprises - the risks of new threats have to be assessed continuously and promptly [2]. Also, appropriate countermeasures have to be taken.

A centralized approach for risk assessment, where this job is carried out by a single organization unit with limited personnel or even a single person, is obviously not practical for large enterprises. A collaborative risk assessment approach, where different persons assess the risks for their domains and the results are later combined, can address the challenge of the size of assessed IT infrastructures. In such an approach multiple persons would independently make

© Springer International Publishing Switzerland 2015
F. Seehusen et al. (Eds.): RISK 2015, LNCS 9488, pp. 34–48, 2015.
DOI: 10.1007/978-3-319-26416-5_3

risk assessments for the parts of the IT infrastructure, which are in their responsibility. All individual risk assessments as well as their results are afterwards combined into an overall assessment.

Such a collaborative approach, however, leads to new challenges. Domain experts with different backgrounds may have different understandings of threats and risks. Especially if inter-connected IT infrastructure components are evaluated by different persons, it is possible that assessments lead to differing or even contradictory results. Also, data from different points of time may result in inconsistent threats ratings.

Our approach to this challenge is to check the validity of the risk assessments and their results. We thereby utilize Semantic Web technologies to integrate risk assessments results with actual information about the IT landscape itself and Markov Logic networks (MLN) to reflect the probabilistic approach of IT risk management.

The paper is structured as follows. Section 2 briefly gives an overview risk assessment, Semantic Web technologies and Markov logic networks. In Sect. 3 we present our approach for validating risk assessment results by using Semantic Web technologies and Markov logic networks. We show the validity of our solution in a case study in Sect. 4 and analyze related works in Sect. 5. We conclude the paper by discussing our work and pointing out the future direction of our work.

2 Background

2.1 IT Risk Management and Risk Assessment

Following the definition of the European Union Agency for Network and Information Security (ENISA) [3], IT risk management has five main processes (see also Fig. 1):

- Definition of Scope: within this process the basic conditions and requirements are defined for the following processes.
- Risk Assessment: this process consists of three activities
  - Risk Identification: creating a list of possible threats
  - Risk Analysis: analyzing the risk level for threats estimating the likelihood and impact of a threat
  - Risk Evaluation: determining if a risk is acceptable or define a treatment priority.
- Risk Treatment: implementing measures against critical risks
- Risk Communication: ensuring the information exchange about risks between decision-makers and other stakeholders
- Monitor and Review: measuring the efficiency and effectiveness of all risk management process

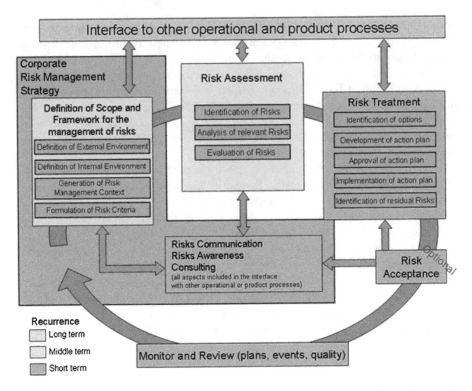

Fig. 1. Overall cycle of a Risk Management process after European Union Agency for Network and Information Security (ENISA) [3]

A more complete overview can be found in survey of the risk assessment methods from the ENISA [3]. Within risk identification data sources such as the "IT-Grundschutz Katalog" [4] provides thorough knowledge about possible threats for IT infrastructure components and possible countermeasures.

2.2 Semantic Web and Ontologies

The idea of Semantic Web is that data should be independent of it presentation and related to one another. This would allow for sharing and reusing data across applications and organization borders. A sound logical basis would make it possible to process the available data within the Internet [5]. Among others, ontologies have been defined as a core technology within the Semantic Web. Ontologies are formal specifications of terms within a specific domain and relations between those terms. They allow for making the semantics of data explicit and accessible to machines.

While the Semantic Web was initially intended as an extension of the World Wide Web, the technologies developed for it are also well-suited for integrating heterogeneous data in organizations. Semantic Web technologies have already been applied to a wide range of applications, from adding semantic metadata for sensors [6] and for enterprise architecture management (EAM) [7].

2.3 Markov Logic Networks (MLN)

Markov logic networks (MLN) apply the idea of Markov Logics to first-order logic. MLN allows to assign weights to the formulas of the first-order logic [9] - i.e. specifying hard and soft formulas. Together with a set of constants, the MLN specifies a probability distribution over possible worlds.

Hard formulas are regular first-order formulas, which have to be fulfilled in every possible world. Soft formulas have weights that support worlds in which they are satisfied, but they do not need to, or in case of negative weights even should not be satisfied. The probability of a possible world, one that satisfies all hard formulas, is proportional to the exponential sum of the weights of the soft formulas that are satisfied in that world. This corresponds to the common representation of Markov networks as log-linear model [9].

An MLN is a template for constructing a Markov network. Figure 2 illustrates the structure of a MLN. For each set of constants, there is a different Markov network, following the rules given in the MLN. Markov logic makes the assumption that different constants refer to different objects (unique name assumption) and the domain consists only of those constant and that no other objects (closed world assumption). An atom is a formula that consists of a single predicate and

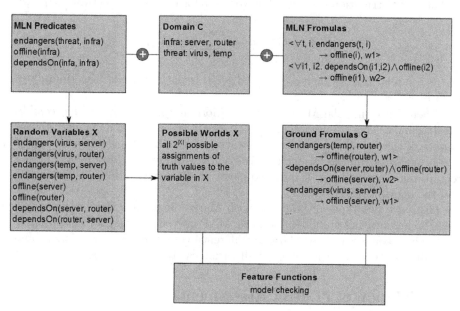

Fig. 2. The diagram describes the grounding of a Markov network. The grounded formulas G are generated by substituting each occurrence of every variable in the MLN Formulas with constants of the domain C. The possible worlds X are generated by giving all possible groundings of each predicate. Both the possible worlds X and the grounded formulas G are checked and provided with a value 1 if there are true and 0 otherwise. (Adapted from [8]).

a grounding substitutes each occurrence of every variable in a formula with a constant. A set of grounded atoms is called a possible world.

An MLN L is a set of pairs $\langle F_i, w_i \rangle$, where F_i is a first-order logic formula and w_i is a real numbered weight [9]. The MLN L, combined with a finite set of constants $C = \{c_1, c_2, ...c_{|C|}\}$, defines a ground Markov network $M_{L,C}$ as follows:

1. $M_{L,C}$ has one binary node for each possible grounding of each predicate in L. The value of the node is 1 if the grounded atom is true and 0 otherwise.
2. $M_{L,C}$ contains one feature for each possible grounding of each formula F_i in L. The value of this feature 1 if the formula is true, and 0 otherwise. The weight of the feature is the w_i associated with F_i in L.

[9, p.113]

Generally, a feature can be any real-valued function of the variables of the network. In this paper we use binary features, essentially making the value of the function equal to the truth value of the grounded atom.

The description as a log-linear model leads to the following definition for the probability distribution over possible worlds x for the Markov network $M_{L,C}$:

$$P(X = x) = \frac{1}{Z} exp\left(\sum_i w_i n_i(x)\right) \tag{1}$$

where Z is a normalization constant and $n_i(x)$ is the number of true groundings of F_i in x.

When describing the MLN we use the format $\langle first\ order\ formula, weight \rangle$. Hard formulas have infinite weights. If the weight is $+\infty$ the formula must always be true, if the weight is $-\infty$ it must always be false. A soft formula with weight 0 has equal probabilities for being satisfied in a world or not. Most query engines require the input to be split into two parts: the formulas (also called program) and the known evidence data.

There are two types of inference with Markov logic: maximum a posteriori (MAP) inference and marginal inference. MAP inference finds the most probable world given some evidence. Marginal inference computes the posteriori probability distribution over the values of all variables given some evidence.

3   Validation of IT Risk Assessments

Collaborative risk assessments in large IT infrastructures may be based on differing or even contradictory assessment for similar threats and dependent components. Thus the overall results may become inconsistent. In order to validate risk assessment we propose to utilize additional information about the IT infrastructure as well as knowledge about threats and their inter-dependencies. Furthermore to reflect the probabilistic approach of risk assessments in a more precise manner we use probabilistic logics for doing the actual validation.

Our approach for the validation of IT risk assessment consists of three steps:

- **Formalizing IT infrastructure and risk assessment results**: create a formal model for risk assessment results and additional information of the IT infrastructure
- **Defining validation rules**: specify business rules to identify anomalies in the given model
- **Detecting anomalies**: utilize Markov Logic networks (MLN) to detect anomalies in given risk assessment results.

3.1   Formalizing IT Infrastructure and Risk Assessment Results

IT risk assessment is considered with estimating the likelihood and impact of threats for IT components. Because neither threats nor IT components are completely isolated from each other, we are convinced that information about their dependencies provide a valuable source to validate risk assessment results. By aligning such information with the risk assessment results we can substantiate the actual assessments with an additional and independent source of knowledge. Especially if risk assessments are carried out collaboratively, not only the work load can be distributed but the assessments of all participants can also be validated against each other.

Enterprise architecture management (EAM), an IT management discipline, provides consolidated information about IT landscapes, the elements therein and their inter-dependencies starting from a business point of view to the actual infrastructure layer. This include information about servers, server locations and network connections within the IT infrastructure.

Catalog of threats, i.e. a list of possible threats for classes of IT components and dependencies between threats are a second relevant information source. "IT-Grundschutz Katalog" [4] provides a thoroughly list of possible threats for IT components. However, it does not include information about dependencies between threats. For example if there is a high likelihood for cable fire there must also be an increased likelihood for fire in the server room.

To integrate both information sources with the actual risk assessment results we create a formal model using ontologies. We therefore build on an ontology for an enterprise architecture [7], which we extend for this approach. We add appropriate details for covering detailed information about the IT infrastructure and include the "IT-Grundschutz Katalog" [4]. To provide an initial set of dependencies between threats we have manually added a number of dependencies. Finally we formalize information elements for risk assessment results. The resulting infrastructure ontology covers information on IT components of the IT infrastructure, possible known threats for standard IT components as well as several threat probabilities as results of risk assessments.

The ontology has been created by using the Web Ontology Language (OWL), which has been standardized by the World Wide Web Consortium (W3C) as an ontology language for the Semantic Web. In particular we choose the QL language profile from the OWL 2 standard, which is optimized for "application that use very large volumes of instance data, and where query answering is the most important reasoning task" [10]. OWL 2 QL is based on the Description Logic DL-Lite$_R$, a decidable fragment of first-order logic, and allows for sound and complete conjunctive query answering in LOGSPACE with respect to the size of instance data. Using this technology provides on the one hand a means to capture and integrate relevant information about IT components and risk assessments. On the other hand such a formalization allows for additional approaches such as validating the risk assessment results using Markov Logic Networks (MLN), which we explain in more detail in the following sections.

3.2 Defining Validation Rules

Having information about IT components, threats and likelihood of threats within a single information base raises the question how to identify anomalies - especially focusing on the likelihood of threats, i.e. the results of risk assessments. Our approach is to define logical rules for validation. These rules reflect available knowledge about possible dependencies, which exist between two IT components and have to be considered appropriate when estimating the likelihood of threats.

For a very first proof of concept, we have identified following dependencies:

- an IT infrastructure component with a high probability for the threat such as "fire" should affect the same threat for all other IT infrastructure components in the same location
- a threat such as "nauthorized access to IT systems" or "malware" should affect other IT infrastructure components in the same network

We can express these dependencies using two universal formulas in the following first-order logic formulas:

$$
\begin{aligned}
&\texttt{hasProbability(infra1, threat1, prob1)} \land \\
&\texttt{hasLocalInfluence(threat1, threat2, prob2)} \land \\
&\texttt{inLocation(infra1, loc)} \land \texttt{inLocation(infra2, loc)} \Rightarrow \\
&\texttt{hasProbability(infra2, threat2, prob2)}
\end{aligned}
\tag{2a}
$$

$$
\begin{aligned}
&\texttt{hasProbability(infra1, threat1, prob1)} \land \\
&\texttt{hasNetworkInfluence (threat1, threat2, prob2)} \land \\
&\texttt{inNetwork (infra1, net)} \land \texttt{inNetwork (infra2, net)} \Rightarrow \\
&\texttt{hasProbability(infra2, threat2, prob2)}
\end{aligned}
\tag{2b}
$$

The formulas have 5 types of variables and 5 predicates. The different types of variables are `infra`[1] as the type of all infrastructure components, `threat` as the type of all threats, `net` as the type of all networks, `loc` as the type of all locations and `prob` as the type of all qualitative probability (like improbable, possible, probable ...). The predicate `hasProbability(infra1, thread1,`

---

[1] In the following we use type writer fonts like `infra` for statements in first-order logic.

prob1) states that a IT infrastructure component `infra1` is endangerd by the threat `threat1` with the probability of occurrence of `prob1`. The predicates `inLocation(infra1, loc)` expressing that a IT infrastructure component `infra1` are located at `loc` and `inNetwork (infra1, net)` respectively that it is connected with the network `net`. `hasLocalInfluence(thread1, thread2, prob1)` and `hasNetworkInfluence (thread1, thread2, prob1)` are two predicates for expressing the local and network influence of a threat. The threat `thread1` influences the occurrence of the threat `thread2` with the probability of `prob1`.

The formula 2a states that if a threat endangers an IT infrastructure component and the threat has a local influence, another IT infrastructure component at the same location is endangered by the second threat with a probability specified in the influence. The second formula, formula 2b is analog to the first, only that it uses network influence instant of location influence. While these threat influences should be universal, the model is a simplification of the reality and it is quite possible that the expert did take some security measure into account which is not represented in our model. Therefore we will not use this as hard formulas, but as soft formulas.

3.3 Detecting Anomalies

Finally, to utilize the collected information on the IT components, the threats and the risk assessment results together with the validation rules we have to translate them into a single MLN program and appropriate evidence.

We use the Formulas 2a and 2b with a weight of 1 and add the following formula:

$$\langle \text{hasInputProbability(infra, thread, prob)} \Rightarrow$$
$$\text{hasProbability(infra, thread, prob)}, 5 \rangle \tag{3}$$

The formula 3 is used to give the result of the risk assertion occurrence probabilities in the evidence a weight, in this case 5, which states that the domain expert most likely did a correct assessment. This weight can be changed to express different confidentiality in the original risk assessment. It is also possible to extend our approached by adding extra predicates to express individual confidentiality. Our full MLN program can be found in Appendix A.

The information in the ontologies can easily be translated into the MLN evidence by using a straightforward rewriting. Examples for MLN evidence can be found in Sect. 4 in Tables 1, 2 and 3.

By using the marginal inference of the MLN, we can calculate the probability of every combination of the `hasProbability` predicate. We then can determine the probability of a threat occurrence on a specific IT infrastructure, by searching the highest `hasProbability` for this IT infrastructure component and threat. If the threat occurrence probability differs from the input then is a possible anomaly and should be further review by the experts.

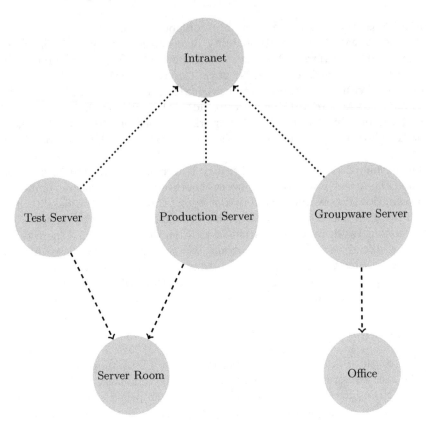

Fig. 3. The IT infrastructure for our case study. Dotted lines represent a connection to a network and dashed lines represent that a component stands in a location.

4   Case Study

We demonstrate the validity our solution with a small use case. Because the creation of ontologies and mapping between them are already covered in other publications, for example [11,12], we focus on the MLN aspects. There are different MLN solvers available, e.g. Alchemy[2], Tuffy[3], and RockIt[4]. Within our work we use the RockIt Solver for our calculations. Our case study has three IT infrastructure components (**Test Server, Production Server** and **Groupware Server**) in two locations (**Server Room** and **Office**) and one network (**Intranet**) (see Fig. 3). We use four occurrence possibility individuals in the following order: **Improbable, Possible, Probable** and **Very Probable**. There are three threats to our IT infrastructure: **Fire, Water** and **Unauthorized Access to IT Systems**. The evidence for our MLN program has three parts.

---

[2] http://alchemy.cs.washington.edu.
[3] http://hazy.cs.wisc.edu/hazy/tuffy.
[4] https://code.google.com/p/rockit.

The first part is the IT infrastructure and the corresponding evidence is listed in Table 1. The second part is the risk assessment we want to check, which is given in Table 2. The last evidence part, see Table 3, defines the influence of the threat occurrence on other threats. We use the MLN program, see Appendix A for the complete program, to calculate the marginal inference.

The Table 4 lists a section of the result, only for the infrastructure Test Server and the threat Fire. Because Possible has the highest probability, with 0.999730, we take it as recommendation from the MLN. Because there is a big gab to the next highest probability, we can assume that the program is very confident in its recommendation. Table 5 lists the result, for each IT infrastructure/threat combination only the occurrence probability with the highest result is given. In five cases the result of the calculation is different from the input, which indicates an anomaly. The possibility for the threat Unauthorized Access to IT Systems changed in all three IT infrastructure components to Probable, which is logical because all three components are in the same network and hacking attacks often propagate through a network. The Test Server and Groupware Server got both a new Water threat with an Improbable probability, because both components have a fire threat. If there is the threat of a fire in a location then it is possible that the extinguishing of a fire results into a water damage. The calculation gives thereby good indicators for invalidity and provides adequate correction recommendations.

Table 1. Evidence Part 1: The IT infrastructure as MLN evidence

```
inLocation("Test Server", "Server Room")
inLocation("Production Server", "Server Room")
inLocation("Groupware Server", "Office")
inNetwork("Test Server", "Intranet")
inNetwork("Production Server", "Intranet")
inNetwork("Groupware Server", "Intranet")
```

Table 2. Evidence Part 2: The result of the risk assessment, which we want to check for invalidity

```
hasInputProbability("Test Server", "Fire", "Possible")
hasInputProbability("Test Server", "Unauthorized Access to IT Systems",
"Very Probable")
hasInputProbability("Production Server", "Fire", "Improbable")
hasInputProbability("Production Server", "Water", "Probable")
hasInputProbability("Production Server", "Unauthorized Access to IT Systems",
"Improbable")
hasInputProbability("Groupware Server", "Fire", "Improbable")
hasInputProbability("Groupware Server", "Unauthorized Access to IT Systems",
"Possible")
```

Table 3. Evidence Part 3: The influence of the threats on each other

```
hasLocalInfluence("Fire", "Fire", "Possible")
hasLocalInfluence("Fire", "Water", "Improbable")
hasNetworkInfluence("Unauthorized Access to IT Systems",
"Unauthorized Access to IT Systems", "Probable")
```

Table 4. The Example of the result of our calculation for the infrastructure `Test Server` and the threat `Fire`

Component	Threat	Occurrence probability	Marginal inference result
Test Server	Fire	Possible	0.999730
Test Server	Fire	Very Probable	0.492144
Test Server	Fire	Probable	0.491708
Test Server	Fire	Improbable	0.490258

5 Related Work

There are other approaches than MLN to combine logic and probability (see [13] for an overview). Because Bayesian networks already used for risk analysis [14], we will limit the discussion of related work to Bayesian logic programs (BLP) [15]. BLP unifies Bayesian networks with logic programming. While MLNs infers all probabilities from a given set of weights, BLP computes the probability for one query from the known probabilities in the resolution to the query statement. MLN has also the advantage that it uses undirected graphs. This has the effect that changes of one weight influence the whole graph and the results. Thereby it is more likely to find new relationships that where not explicitly modeled. This has on the other hand the disadvantage that it is harder to isolate a single variable. MLNs have been used for a wide range of problems, for instance in data integration [16] and determine the availability of IT infrastructure components [17].

While there are already approaches for finding errors in ontologies [18], there is more work needed to make these methods applicable in practice [19]. They are also limited by the expressiveness of the ontology language; therefore it is not possible to use soft formulas as indicators for finding errors. The combination of Semantic Web and Markov Logic Networks is also nothing new. It has already been used for link prediction and collective classification, for filling in missing attributes and relationships; entity resolution, for matching equivalent entities that have different names; information extraction, for adding structure to raw or semi-structured text [20].

6 Discussion

To our knowledge this paper presents a novel solution for finding anomalies in risk assessments. We utilize Semantic Web technologies to formalize different

Table 5. The results of our calculation, only the most probable threat occurrence probability is given for each infrastructure threat combination.

Component	Threat	Input probability	Highest marginal inference probability
Test Server	Unauthorized Access to IT Systems	Very Probable	Probable
Test Server	Fire	Possible	Possible
Test Server	Water	-	Improbable
Production Server	Unauthorized Access to IT Systems	Improbable	Probable
Production Server	Fire	Improbable	Improbable
Production Server	Water	Probable	Probable
Groupware Server	Unauthorized Access to IT Systems	Possible	Probable
Groupware Server	Fire	Improbable	Improbable
Groupware Server	Water	-	Improbable

relevant data sources. Markov logic networks allows for detecting contradictory assessments and compute corrections. We have defined rules to validate the probability of threat occurrences and specified additional information sources relevant to the validation. We have shown the validity of our approach in a small case study.

Our solution has following advantages. By using Semantic Web technologies, i.e. an ontology, we describe the IT all relevant information elements and their dependencies and integrate data from EAM and risk assessments into such information graph. Such an information graph provides a solid foundation for analysis but also for additional means of support such a the automated validation of risk assessments.

We compute the marginal inference of the MLN model to get the probability distribution of all the variables. Comparing them with the actual risk assessment results leads to possible anomalies in the estimation of likelihood of threats. Moreover, by using MLN we can not only detect possible anomalies but also computer the most probable value. While it would be possible to use MAP for our approach, it would only provide the most probable world and no information about how probable other alternatives are.

The used rules for threat and location dependencies furthermore can not only be given as hard formulas but also as soft formulas. Such soft rules reflect the knowledge of domain experts in a more realistic manner. The MLN model also allows for circular dependencies within components of the IT infrastructure and threats, which are quite common in real world scenarios. The weights used with the soft formulas can also be determined automatically using existing learning approaches [9]. It is therefore possible to iterative train the weights of the MLN by accepting or rejecting the suggested changes of the MLN calculation.

There are some limitations to our solution. The modeling with MLN is not as straight forward as the simple representation suggests [8]. The relationship between weights and the probabilities of the marginal inference result can be counterintuitive. The probability depends on the whole MLN, the program and the evidence, and even the number of individual can have an effect. The weight of a soft formula therefore does not directly correspond to a specific universal probability for this formula. Changing the weights in one formula shifts the relative weights of the possible worlds where the formula is true. This can affect the probability of variables which are not directly connected to the formula. This is the reason why we don't express the threat occurrence probability directly with weights but with constants. If we express the threat occurrence probability with weights, this would result very many weights. These would affect each other and it would be very hard to find the correct corresponding weights for the threat occurrence probability.

The scalability of our approach needs to be further investigated. While the OWL2-QL profile has a very good scalability, we need to test the MLN inference with bigger data sets. The marginal inference with MLN has the advantage that it uses a Gibbs sampling approach. The Gibbs sampling gets more accurate with each sample and it allows us thereby to choose how much time to invest into the accuracy of the probabilities.

Our approach does not use the order of the threat occurrence probability. It returns the probability with is supported by the most weights, but it does not find compromise solutions. If there is weight for a high and a low probability our approach returns the one with more weight and not a medium probability.

7   Conclusion

In this paper we have described an approach to find anomalies in collaborative risk assessments. Our solution aims at improving the confidence in collaborative risk assessments by detecting contradictory assessments of threats for same or dependent infrastructure components. First, we combine and integrate relevant information about the IT infrastructure itself, threats and their interdependencies as well as various risk assessments into a single formal model. We therefore utilize Semantic Web technologies which allows for the integration of heterogeneous data sources. We finally translate the resulting model into a Markov Logic network and compute the marginal inference to detect anomalies in risk assessments and to determine more probable assessments for risks.

While we have focused our work in this paper primarily on the probability of threat occurrences, future work may also consider threat impact and criticality. Also, we plan to research the use of additional confidence values that may be collected from the assessors during the identification of risks. This would provide us with an additional source for aligning collaborative risk assessments.

Acknowledgement. This work has been partially supported by the German Federal Ministry of Economics and Technology (BMWI) in the framework of the Central Innovation Program SME (Zentrales Innovationsprogramm Mittelstand - ZIM) within the project "Risk management tool for complex IT infrastructures".

A   RockIt MLN

For our MLN, we use the syntax of RockIt [21]. RockIt expects first order formulas in conjunctive normal form (CNF). An online version of RockIt is available here: http://executor.informatik.uni-mannheim.de/systems/rockit/

```
*inNetwork(infra, net)
*inLocation(infra, loc)
*hasInputProbability(infra, thread, prob)
hasProbability(infra, thread, prob)
*hasLocalInfluence(thread, thread, prob)
*hasNetworkInfluence(thread, thread, prob)

5 !hasInputProbability(infra, thread, prob) v
  hasProbability(infra, thread, prob)

1 !hasProbability(infra1, thread1, prob1) v
  !hasLocalInfluence(thread1, thread2, prob2) v
  !inLocation(infra1, loc) v !inLocation(infra2,  loc) v
  hasProbability(infra2, thread2, prob2)

1 !hasProbability(infra1, thread1, prob1) v
  !hasNetworkInfluence(thread1, thread2, prob2) v
  !inNetwork(infra1, net) v !inNetwork(infra2, net) v
  hasProbability(infra2, thread2, prob2)
```

References

1. Zambon, E., Etalle, S., Wieringa, R.J., Hartel, P.: Model-based qualitative risk assessment for availability of it infrastructures. Softw. Syst. Model. **10**(4), 553–580 (2011)
2. IBM X-Force: Mid-year trend and risk report 2013. Technical report, IBM X-Force (2013)
3. Technical Department of ENISA Section Risk Management: ENISA: Risk management: implementation principles and inventories for risk management/risk assessment methods and tools. Technical report, European Network and Information Security Agency (ENISA) (2006)
4. Bundesamt für Sicherheit in der Informationstechnik: IT-Grundschutz-Kataloge. Technical report, Bundesamt für Sicherheit in der Informationstechnik (2013)
5. Berners-Lee, T., Hendler, J., Lassila, O., et al.: The semantic web. Sci. Am. **284**(5), 28–37 (2001)

6. Sheth, A., Henson, C., Sahoo, S.S.: Semantic sensor web. IEEE Internet Comput. **12**(4), 78–83 (2008)
7. Chen, W., Hess, C., Langermeier, M., Stülpnagel, J., Diefenthaler, P.: Semantic enterprise architecture management. In: ICEIS, vol. 3, pp. 318–325 (2013)
8. Jain, D.: Knowledge engineering with markov logic networks: a review. In: Beierle, C., Kern-Isberner, G. (eds.) Evolving Knowledge in Theory and Applications. Informatik-Bericht, vol. 361, pp. 16–30. Fakultät für Mathematik und Informatik, FernUniversität, Hagen (2011)
9. Richardson, M., Domingos, P.: Markov logic networks. Mach. Learn. **62**(1–2), 107–136 (2006)
10. Motik, B., Grau, B., Horrocks, I., Wu, Z., Fokoue, A., Lutz, C.: OWL 2 web ontology language: Profiles. W3C recommendation (2012)
11. Kalfoglou, Y., Schorlemmer, M.: Ontology mapping: the state of the art. Knowl. Eng. Rev. **18**(01), 1–31 (2003)
12. Braun, S., Schmidt, A., Walter, A., Nagypal, G., Zacharias, V.: Ontology maturing: a collaborative web 2.0 approach to ontology engineering. In: Noy, N., Alani, H., Stumme, G., Mika, P., Sure, Y., Vrandecic, D. (eds.): Proceedings of the Workshop on Social and Collaborative Construction of Structured Knowledge (CKC 2007) at the 16th International World Wide Web Conference (WWW2007), CEUR Workshop Proceedings, 8 May 2007, Banff, Canada, vol. 273 (2007)
13. Braz, R., Amir, E., Roth, D.: A survey of first-order probabilistic models. In: Holmes, D., Jain, L. (eds.) Innovations in Bayesian Networks. SCI vol. 156, pp. 289–317. Springer, Berlin Heidelberg (2008)
14. Weber, P., Medina-Oliva, G., Simon, C., Iung, B.: Overview on Bayesian networks applications for dependability, risk analysis and maintenance areas. Eng. Appl. Artif. Intell. **25**(4), 671–682 (2012)
15. Kersting, K., De Raedt, L.: Bayesian logic programs. CoRR cs.AI/0111058 (2001)
16. Niepert, M., Noessner, J., Meilicke, C., Stuckenschmidt, H.: Probabilistic-logical web data integration. In: Polleres, A., d'Amato, C., Arenas, M., Handschuh, S., Kroner, P., Ossowski, S., Patel-Schneider, P. (eds.) Reasoning Web 2011. LNCS, vol. 6848, pp. 504–533. Springer, Heidelberg (2011)
17. von Stülpnagel, J., Ortmann, J., Schoenfisch, J.: IT risk management with Markov logic networks. In: Jarke, M., Mylopoulos, J., Quix, C., Rolland, C., Manolopoulos, Y., Mouratidis, H., Horkoff, J. (eds.) CAiSE 2014. LNCS, vol. 8484, pp. 301–315. Springer, Heidelberg (2014)
18. Parsia, B., Sirin, E., Kalyanpur, A.: Debugging owl ontologies. In: Proceedings of the 14th International Conference on World Wide Web, pp. 633–640. ACM (2005)
19. Stuckenschmidt, H.: Debugging owl ontologies-a reality check. In: EON (2008)
20. Domingos, P., Lowd, D., Kok, S., Poon, H., Richardson, M., Singla, P.: Uncertainty Reasoning for the Semantic Web I. Springer, Heidelberg (2008)
21. Noessner, J., Niepert, M., Stuckenschmidt, H.: Rockit: Exploiting parallelism and symmetry for map inference in statistical relational models. In: des Jardins, M., Littman, M. (eds.) Proceedings of the Twenty-Seventh AAAI Conference on Artificial Intelligence, July 14–18, 2012, Bellevue, Washington, USA. AAAI Press (2013)

CyVar: Extending Var-At-Risk to ICT

Fabrizio Baiardi$^{(\boxtimes)}$, Federico Tonelli, and Alessandro Bertolini

Dipartimento di Informatica, Università di Pisa, Pisa, Italy
{baiardi,tonelli}@di.unipi.it

Abstract. CyVar extends the Value-At-Risk statistics to ICT systems under attack by intelligent, goal oriented agents. CyVar is related to the time it takes an agent to acquire some access privileges and to the one it owns these privileges. To evaluate the former time, we use the security stress, a synthetic measure of the robustness of an ICT system. We approximate this measure through the Haruspex suite, an integrated set of tools that supports ICT risk assessment and management. After defining CyVar, we show how it supports the evaluation of three versions of an industrial control system.

Keywords: Risk assessment · Value at risk · Impact assessment

1 Introduction

Volatility is a popular measure of risk even if it neglects movement direction: a stock can be volatile because it suddenly jumps higher. Value-At-Risk is a more appropriate risk measure because it focuses on the most significant information for investors, the odds of losing money. This statistics has three components: a time period t, a confidence level c and a loss amount l and it defines, with a confidence c, the probability of losing more than l in t.

CyVar generalizes Value-At-Risk to information and communication technology, ICT, and it assumes a threat model where intelligent agents aim to achieve some predefined goals through chained exploits, i.e. through a sequence of attacks. Each attack in a sequence escalates the privileges, e.g. access rights, of the agent till it owns all those in one of its goals. The resulting impact is a function of the time the agent takes to acquire the rights in a goal and of the one it owns these rights. CyVar computes the former through the *security stress*, the probability that an agent reaches a goal in a given time. We approximate this stress through the Haruspex suite, a set of tools that supports a model based assessment of ICT risk. The suite tools apply a Monte Carlo method to build a statistical sample and use it to compute the statistics to support the assessment.

We structure this paper as follows. Section 2 briefly reviews related work. Section 3 outlines the Haruspex methodology and the tools of the Haruspex suite of interest. Section 4 introduces the security stress and its approximation through the Haruspex suite. Then, it discusses alternative definitions of the impact function. Section 5 defines the CyVar statistics and applies it to evaluate alternative versions of an industrial control system. Lastly, we draw some conclusions.

© Springer International Publishing Switzerland 2015
F. Seehusen et al. (Eds.): RISK 2015, LNCS 9488, pp. 49–62, 2015.
DOI: 10.1007/978-3-319-26416-5_4

2   Related Works

In [1–5] describe the tools of the Haruspex suite, their validation and how they automate the assessment and the management of the risk due to an ICT system. The simulation of the agent attacks that is the foundation of the suite is discussed in [6–9]. In [10] discusses attack and defense modeling for critical infrastructures. Baiardi, et al. [11] defines the security stress.

The metrics in [12–14] evaluate the robustness of an ICT infrastructure under attack without integrating the proposed metrics with the simulation of the attacks. The metric in [15] is focused on the discovery of zero-day vulnerabilities. In [16–19] review alternative security metrics. Pamula, et al. [20] is similar to the security stress as it considers the amount of work to attack a system. Böhme [21] investigate the relation between security metrics and security investment. Gordon and Loeb [22] analyzes the optimal security investment. Kundur, et al. [23] evaluates the impact of attacks against smartgrids.

3   The Haruspex Approach to Risk Assessment

We outline how Haruspex methodology assesses ICT risk and describe the suite that supports this methodology.

3.1   The Haruspex Methodology

Haruspex[1] is a model based methodology to assess the risk in a scenario where intelligent agents attack an ICT system to acquire some access rights and control some system modules. Being intelligent, these agents minimize their efforts to reach their goals. The first step of an assessment defines the model of the target system and those of the agents in the considered scenario. These models are defined in terms of simple and easily measurable factors, such as the success probability of a single attack. Then, the assessment executes the models and let they interact to simulate the joint evolution of the system and of the agents in the original scenario. The simulation preserves the overall complexity in the scenario. By observing this evolution, the assessment discovers whether and how each agent reaches its goals. Haruspex handles randomness in the evolution by applying a Monte Carlo method and it builds a statistical sample by collecting information in multiple, independent simulations of the evolution. The assessment uses this sample to compute the statistics of interest, such as the probability that an agent reaches its goal. Haruspex supports a *security-by-design approach* because it only needs the models of the system and of the agents to produce a statistical sample to compute statistics of interest. As a consequence, the risk a system poses can be assessed and managed before its actual deployment.

---

[1] An ancient Tuscany forecaster.

3.2   Modeling a System and the Agents

Haruspex models the ICT system that is the target of an assessment as a set of interconnected modules. Each module defines some operations that the users or the other components can invoke provided that they own the proper privileges. The vulnerabilities, i.e. the defects, in a module enable some attacks. An attack consists of some actions an agent executes to illegally acquire some privileges and it is described through some attributes. Two attributes describe, respectively, the set of privileges an agent needs to execute the attack and the privileges the agent acquires if the attack succeeds. Other attributes include the success probability and the time to execute the attack. The success probability depends upon both the agent and some structural properties of the attack. The model of the target system describes the system modules, their vulnerabilities and the attacks the vulnerabilities enable. Some of these vulnerabilities are suspected and the agents may discover them in the future. Each suspected vulnerability is paired with the probability agents discover it at a given time. Suspected vulnerabilities support a *what-if* approach to analyze how a new vulnerability affects the overall risk.

The Haruspex model of an agent describes its legal privileges, its goals, the information on the target system it can access and how it selects and implements sequences of attacks to reach a goal. A goal is a set of privileges the agent wants to acquire. In general, this requires a sequence of attacks because no single attack grants all the privileges in a goal. Each attack in a sequence escalates the agent privileges and it enables the execution of further attacks to acquire further privileges till the agent acquires all those in a goal.

The accuracy of the modeling of how each agent selects the sequence of attacks it implements strongly influences the one of the overall evolution. To increase this accuracy, Haruspex pairs each agent with attributes such as the *look-ahead*, a non negative integer, and the *selection strategy*. The look-ahead that defines how the agent evaluates the future benefits when ranking alternative sequences. An agent with a zero look-ahead randomly selects the attacks in its sequence. Otherwise, the agent ranks all the sequences with a number of attacks bounded its look-ahead to select the one to implement. If some of these sequences lead to a goal, then the selection strategy always returns one of these sequences. Otherwise, the look-ahead is too low to discover sequences leading to a goal and the strategy ranks sequences according to the attributes of their attacks. The ranking may consider, among others, the success probability or the time to implement a sequence or the number of rights the agent acquires. Haruspex pairs each agent with one of the predefined selection strategies it supports.

3.3   The Haruspex Suite

The Haruspex suite is an integrated set of tools that support the proposed methodology. Its kernel consists of three tools: the *builder*, the *descriptor* and the *engine*. The first two tools build the models of, respectively, the system and an agent. The *engine* uses these models to apply a Monte Carlo method that runs multiple simulation of the agent attacks.

The suite includes other tools. As an example, the *manager* uses the output of the *engine* to select cost effective countermeasures that minimize the risk. The tools interact through a shared database that stores the models of interest and the samples the *engine* returns. In the following, we briefly describe the *engine*.

The *engine* retrieves in the shared database the models of the target system and those of the agents in the scenario of interest. Using these models, it implements a Haruspex experiment with multiple independent *runs*. Each run simulates the behavior of the agents and of the system for the same time interval. At the beginning of a run, each agent owns its legal privileges only. A run ends either when all the agents reach one of their goals or at the end of the time interval. At each time step, the *engine* determines the suspected vulnerabilities the agents discover. Then, it considers each idle agent and it invokes the agent strategy to select the sequence it implements. The agent is busy for the time to select a sequence plus the one to implement its first q attacks. q is the agent *continuity*, the number of attacks it implements before invoking against its selection strategy. Agents with a low continuity exploit at best newly discovered vulnerabilities at the cost of a larger selection overhead.

The time to select a sequence also includes the one an agent spends to collect information on the vulnerabilities that enable the attacks in the sequences it ranks. The *engine* determines the success of an attack according to the attack attributes and, if it is successful, it grants the corresponding privileges to the agent. An agent repeats a failed attack for a number of time equal to its *persistence*, a further agent attribute. An agent is idle when it does not own the privileges to implement any attack and it may leave this state only after the discovery of a suspected vulnerability.

At the end of a run, the *engine* collects distinct observations on the sequence each agent has implemented, on the components it has attacked and on the goal it has reached. The observations populate a database to compute the statistics of interest. The confidence level of these statistics increases with the number of runs in the experiment because each run produces one observation in the collected sample. The *engine* starts a new run till some predefined statistics reaches the required confidence level. The parameter of the confidence level depends upon the information of interest. As an example, to discover all the sequences an agent may implement, the parameter of interest is the set of system modules an agent attacks. An alternative parameter is the time it takes an agent to reach a goal.

4   Security Stress and Impact Function

This section introduces two auxiliary functions to define CyVar: the security stress and the impact. The former evaluates the robustness of a system with respect to an agent. Instead, the impact evaluates the loss of the owner as a function of the time an agent owns the rights in a goal. In the following, we denote an agent by ag, by sg the goals of ag, and by g one of the goals in sg.

4.1   Security Stress

$Str_{ag,sg}^{S}(t)$ the security stress of a system S at t due to ag that aims to reach a goal in sg is the probability that ag reaches a goal in sg within t. Being a probability distribution, $Str_{ag,sg}^{S}(t)$ is monotone, non decreasing in t and $Str_{ag,sg}^{S}(0) = 0$. $Str_{ag,g}^{S}$ is a synthetic evaluation of the robustness of S because its shape is related to critical attributes of S. To discuss this relation, we define two times:

1. t_0 is the lowest time such that $Str_{ag,sg}^{S}(t) > 0$,
2. t_1 is the lowest time such that $Str_{ag,sg}^{S}(t) = 1$.

Let us assume that both times exist. If we consider ag as a force trying to change the shape of S, then this force is ineffective till t_0. Then, the attacks of ag change the shape of S that cracks after t_1 because ag is always successful for larger times. $t_1 - t_0$ evaluates how long S can resist, at least partially, to the attacks of ag before cracking.

t_0 depends upon both the time to execute an attack and the length of the shortest attack sequence to reach g. t_1 depends upon the success probability of attacks in the sequences leading to g that determines the average number of times ag repeats at before it succeeds. $t_1 - t_0$ depends upon both the standard deviation of the lengths of the sequences to g and the success probabilities of their attacks. These dependencies show that $Str_{ag,sg}^{S}(t)$ evaluates the robustness of S in a more accurate way than metrics that consider just a single value, such as the average time or the average number of attacks to reach g.

The function $Sur_{ag,sg}^{S}(t) = 1 - Str_{ag,sg}^{S}(t)$ is a survival function [24] that plots the probability that S survives to the attacks of ag to reach a goal in sg.

We approximate $Str_{ag,g}^{S}(t)$ as the percentage of runs in an *engine* experiment where ag reaches g before t. The experiment simulates ag for at least t and it reaches the confidence level of interest on the time ag takes to reach g. This confidence level is also the one of the approximation of $Str_{ag,g}^{S}$.

If the agents in sa share the goals in sg, then the stress $Str_{sa,sg}^{S}(t)$ due to these agents is the one of the most dangerous agent in sa. This agent, if it exists, is the one that always reaches a goal before any other one so that it results in a stress larger than those of other agents.

The definition of the security stress due to a set of agent is not interesting when the agents have distinct goals because in this case they also have distinct motivations and result in distinct impacts. However, we may define the corresponding stress as the weighted average of the stresses due to each agent. The weight of an agent evaluates its contribution to the overall impact. The remainder of the paper only considers the stress due to agents with the same goals.

4.2   Impact Function

The impact due to an agent that reaches a goal strongly depends upon the target system and upon the agent motivations. We discuss in the following how these features determine the shape of the impact function.

$Imp_{ag,g}^S(t)$ defines the loss for the owner of S due to ag as a function of t, the time ag owns the rights in g. $Imp_{ag,g}^S(t)$ is monotone non decreasing in t, $Imp_{ag,g}^S(0) = 0$ and its shape depends upon the motivations of ag.

Suppose, as an example, that ag aims to steal some intellectual property value, e.g. the design of a component or the source code of a software system. Here ag is interested in acquiring the privilege of reading some information in S. After reaching this goal, ag needs some time, say t_s, to steal some information. The exfiltration of information starts as soon as ag reaches g, then $Imp_{ag,g}^S(t)$ increases as long as t lies in the interval $0..t_s$ and it is constant for larger values. The second order derivative of $Imp_{ag,g}^S$ is strictly negative in $0..t_s$ due to the decreasing contribution to the overall loss of further information that ag exfiltrates. In more complex scenarios, the second order derivative increases for values of t in $0..t_{s1}$ and decreases if t lies in $t_{s1}..t_s$ because, initially, the contribution of further information increases the loss.

The value of t_s depends upon the amount of information to exfiltrate as well as upon ag risk tolerance. t_s is inversely related to the risk tolerance of ag because, in most systems, the probability of detecting the exfiltration increases with the relative communication bandwidth of S when it exploits. Hence, ag can reduce the exfiltration time at the cost of using a large percentage of available bandwidth and of a larger probability of discovering the exfiltration. Similar impact functions apply if ag aims to destroy some data. Now ag has to acquire the privilege of updating this data and then it overwrites them with some garbage. Now, t_s is the time to overwrite the data of interest. Another important feature to determine t_s is whether the overwrite has to be stealthy.

Let us assume now that S is an industrial control system, ICS, and that ag attacks it to replace the owner of S in the control of the plan production or to damage the plan itself. Stuxnet is a well known example of the latter [25, 26]. If ag aims to control the production, the first order derivative of $Imp_{ag,g}^S(t)$ is constant and the second order one is zero. The same function applies even to the stealing of intellectual property anytime S steadily produces new information to steal. When, instead, ag aims to sabotage the plan, $Imp_{ag,g}^S(t)$ steadily increases till it reaches a threshold value t_d and is constant for larger times. The second order derivative increases in the interval $0..t_d$ if the cost of recovering the loss due to ag increases with the time ag has available.

5   CyVar: Value at Risk for ICT

CyVar extends the Value-At-Risk statistics to the risk due to the attacks of goal oriented agents against an ICT system. After defining CyVar for one agent with one goal, we extend this definition to alternative goals and then to some agents with the same or with distinct goals. Here and in the following, we do not explicitly discuss the confidence level of CyVar as it is the one of the Haruspex experiments to generate the sample to compute CyVar. Furthermore, we assume that all the agents in a scenario attack the target system S simultaneously.

5.1   CyVar: One Agent with One Goal

Given an impact function $Imp^S_{ag,g}(t)$, $CyVar^S_{ag,g}(v_q, t_q)$ is the probability of a loss larger than v_q in the interval $0..t_q$ due to ag that aims to reach g. To compute $CyVar^S_{ag,g}(v_q, t_q)$, first of all we compute t_i where $Imp^S_{ag,g}(t_i) = v_q$ as the minimum of the set Sle that includes any t_h where $Imp^S_{ag,g}(t_h) \geq v_q$. If Sle is empty, then $CyVar^S_{ag,g}(v_q, t_q) = 0$, e.g. the loss cannot be larger than v_q. Otherwise, t_i exists and $CyVar^S_{ag,g}(v_q, t_q)$ is the probability that ag owns the rights in g for at least t_i. In turn, this probability is equal to the one that ag reaches g in an interval bounded by $t_q - t_i$. Hence,

$$CyVar^S_{ag,g}(v_q, t_q) = Str^S_{ag,g}(t_q - t_i).$$

Informally, we compute $CyVar^S_{ag,g}(v_q, t_q)$ by inverting the impact function to discover how long ag should own the rights in g to produce a loss v_q. Using this interval, we compute the one ag has available to reach g. Obviously, the longer the time ag should own the rights, the shorter the interval of time it has available to reach g and the smaller the value of $CyVar^S_{ag,g}(v_q, t_q)$. We assume that S does not include intrusion detection mechanisms to detect that an agent has reached a goal. If S includes these mechanisms, it may discover successful attacks and reduce the time ag owns the rights in g. In turn, this reduces the time ag has available to reach a goal and it increases the resulting stress.

As an example, suppose that $Imp^S_{ag,g}(t) = \alpha \cdot t^2$. To discover the probability of a loss larger than β in interval $0..\gamma$, we compute the time ag should own the rights in g to produce this loss. This time has to be larger than $\sqrt{\beta/\alpha}$. Hence, the probability of a larger loss is the one that ag reaches g in less than $t = \gamma - \sqrt{\beta/\alpha}$. If t is larger than zero, the probability of interest is the value of the security stress at t. Hence,

$$CyVar^S_{ag,g}(\beta, \gamma) = Str^S_{ag,g}(\gamma - \sqrt{\beta/\alpha})$$

5.2   CyVar: One Agent with Alternative Goals

Let us suppose now that ag aims to reach any goal in $sg = \{g_1, ..., g_n\}$. For each goal g_i in sg the assessment defines the corresponding impact function $Imp^S_{ag,g,i}(t)$. To compute $CyVar^S_{ag,sg}(v_q, t_q)$, we compute $CyVar^S_{ag,g_i}(v_q, t_q)$ for each g_i in sg, i.e. we compute the probability that a loss larger than v_q occurs because ag reaches g_i. The corresponding stress function takes into into account g_i only. Hence, for each g_i in sg, we implement a distinct experiment where each run ends only when and if ag reaches g_i. Since the worst outcome for the owner is the largest value of $CyVar^S_{ag,g_i}(v_q, t_q)$, we have that:

$$CyVar^S_{ag,sg}(v_q, t_q) = max\left\{CyVar^S_{ag,g_i}(v_q, t_q), \forall g_i \in sg\right\}.$$

The computation is strongly simplified if all the goals in sg share the same impact function. Under this condition, we only need one experiment to approximate the security stress because each run ends when ag reaches any of its goals.

5.3 CyVar: Agents with Alternative Goals

We define CyVar for a set sa with k agents, $sa = \{ag_1, ..., ag_k\}$ and a set $sg = \{sg_1, ..., sg_k\}$ where sg_j is the set with the goals of sa_j. In the following, we assume agents in sa are *independent* so that no agent delays the other ones and the overall impact is the sum of those of each agent.

To compute $CyVar^S_{sa,sg}(v_q, t_q)$ we decompose v_q into k non negative values, i.e. any set $dv = \{dv_1, ..., dv_k\}$ where

1. $\forall j \in 1..k, dv_j \geq 0$ and
2. $\sum_{j=1,k} dv_j = v_q$.

For each decomposition dv, $pr(dv)$ is the joint probability that each agent in sa results in a loss larger that the corresponding one in dv. $pr(vd)$ is the product of the probabilities that the loss due to sa_j is larger than dv_j because agents are independent. For each agent sa_j, dv_j is one if $d_j = 0$ and it is equal to $CyVar^S_{sa_j,sg_j}(dv_j, t_q)$ otherwise. To compute $CyVar^S_{sa,sg}(v_q, t_q)$, we consider the set Sv with any decomposition of v_q:

$$CyVar^S_{sa,sg}(v_q, t_q) = \sum_{sd \in Sv} pr(sd).$$

In other words, to compute the probability of a loss larger than v_q with reference to sa and sg, we sum the probabilities of alternative decompositions of v_q among the agents in sa.

6 An Example

This section applies CyVar to three versions of an ICS that supervises and controls power generation. By considering three versions of the same system we also show how the proposed statistics is related to the structure of a system.

6.1 The Three Versions

Any version of the ICS of interest is an ICT network segmented into four types of subnets: Central, Power Context, Process and Control.

Users of the intranet run the business processes of power generation through the nodes in a Central subnet. The plant operators interact with the SCADA servers through the nodes in a Power Context subnet. The SCADA servers and the systems to control power production belongs to a Process network. Finally, the ICS drives the plant production through some programmable logical components, PLCs, in a Control subnet.

$S1$, the first version of the ICS [27] includes 49 nodes segmented into six subnets, see Fig. 1. The Central subnet includes 24 nodes, the Power Context includes 7 nodes. Then, Process subnet 1 and 2 include, respectively, 9 and 7 nodes. Each Process subnet is connected to a Control subnet with one PLC. Three nodes connect the Central subnet to the Power Context one. Two pairs

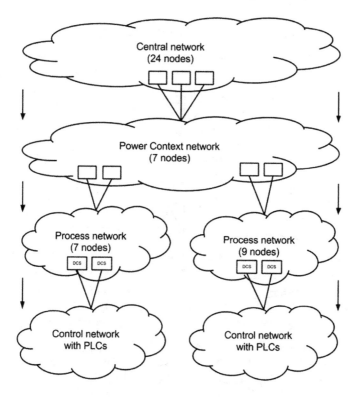

Fig. 1. First version of the ICS

of nodes in the Power Context network are connected to those in one Process subnet. Lastly, two nodes in each Process subnet are connected to the corresponding Control subnet. $S2$, the second version of the ICS doubles the number of nodes by replicating each node without altering the number of connections between subnets. Figure 2 shows the third version $S3$. While $S3$ includes the same number of nodes than $S2$ (98 nodes), it is a more accurate implementation of the *defence-in-depth* strategy because it splits the Central subnet into two subnets with 24 nodes each. Furthermore, only one of the resulting subnets is connected to the Power Context subnets.

6.2 The Agents and Their Impact

We assume that the agents attack the ICS to control the production plan and reduces the efficiency of the overall production. Our definition of the impact function assumes that the owner of S loses Low for each unit of time an agent controls one PLC and that the loss increases with the number of PLCs the agents controls. The corresponding impact function is $\sum_i Low \cdot t_i$ where t_i is the time the agents controls the i-th PLC. In the following we use hours as time units.

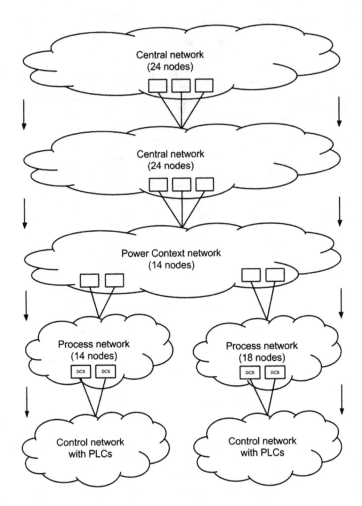

Fig. 2. Third version of the ICS

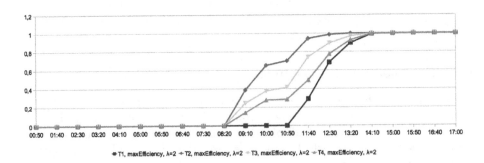

Fig. 3. First version: stress curve of the most dangerous agents

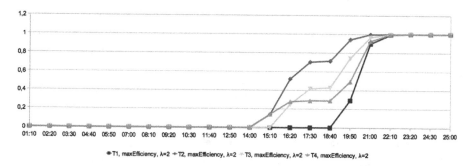

Fig. 4. Second version: stress curve of the most dangerous agents

In the scenario of interest, any agent initially owns some rights on a node in the Central subnet and it aims to control some PLCs. We consider four classes of agents, $T1, ..., T4$. The goal $g1$ of $T1$ agents is the control of both the PLCs in the ICS. Instead, the goal $g2$ of $T2$ agents is the control of any of the PLCs. $g3$ and $g4$ the goals of agents in, respectively, the classes $T3$ and $T4$ is the control of one, predefined PLC. As a consequence, the impact due to a $T1$ agent is $2 \cdot Low \cdot t$ while the one of any other agent is $Low \cdot t$. Each class includes seven agents that differ in the strategy to select the attack sequence.

6.3   CyVar for the Three Versions

For each ICS version, Figs. 3, 4, and 5 show the stress curves of the most dangerous agent in each class. The confidence level of these curve is 95 %. The figures show that in $S1$, the most dangerous $T2$ agent reaches $g2$ in about twelve hours while any agent of another class reaches its goal in about fourteen hours, i.e. about two hours later. The most dangerous agent for $S2$ is a $T2$ agent that reaches $g2$ in about 21 h. Other agents take one more hour. The time it takes each agent to reach its goal in $S3$ is a bit larger than in $S2$. Indeed, a $T2$ agent reaches $g2$ only 20 min later than in $S2$ but the remaining agents reach their goal after more than two hours. As expected, $S1$ is the most fragile version due to the low number of attacks to reach a goal. The number of nodes in $S2$ confuses the agents and increases the time to reach their goal. Finally, $S3$ is the more robust one because the numbers of nodes and of subnets increase the number of attacks and the time to reach a goal.

Let us assume that $Low = 10$ and that we are interested in values of CyVar for agents in four classes $T1, ..., T4$ if $V = 100$ and $t = 24$ h.

The impact of agent ag in the $T1$ class is equal to V if it owns the rights in $g1$ for $V/(2 \cdot Low) = 100/20 = 5$ h. This requires that ag reaches $g1$ in less than 19 h. In $S1$, the most dangerous $T1$ agent always reaches $g1$ in less than 19 h. Hence, $CyVar^{S1}_{ag,g1}(100, 24) = 1$ and the owner will suffer this loss in 24 h anytime this agent attacks $S1$. The situation strongly changes in $S2$ where the probability that a $T1$ agent results in this loss lies in the range $[0.2..0.3]$. Lastly, $CyVar^{S3}_{ag,s}(100, 24) = 0$ because a T1 agent cannot reach $g1$ in 19 h.

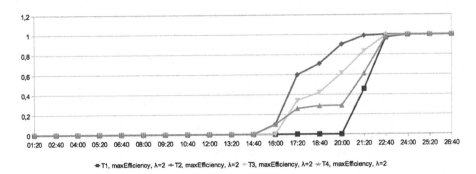

Fig. 5. Third version: stress curve of the most dangerous agents

An agent ag that belongs to the $T2$ class results in an impact V if it owns the rights in $g2$ for 10 h. Hence, ag should reach $g2$ in less than 14 h. In $S1$, this happens with a probability 1, e.g. $CyVar_{ag,g}^{S1}(100, 24) = 1$ while both in $S2$ and $S3$ this never happens, e.g. $CyVar_{ag,g2}^{S2}(100, 24) = CyVar_{ag,g2}^{S3}(100, 24) = 0$. Similar considerations apply to $T3$ and $T4$ agents. Both these agents take more time to reach their goal than a $T2$ agent that freely chooses the PLC to control.

Consider now a set sa with one $T3$ agent and a $T4$ one and assume they attack the ICS simultaneously. Since each agent aims to control a distinct PLC, they are independent, i.e. each agent does not affect the other one, and their overall impact is the sum of their impacts. Hence, these agents result in an impact V if the sum of the times they own the rights in, respectively, $g3$ and $g4$ is larger than 10 h. Let us consider a decomposition where each agent owns these rights for at least 5 h. This implies that each agent reaches its goal in less that 19 h. This happens with a probability 1 in $S1$, e.g. $CyVar_{sa,sg}^{S1}(100, 24) = 1$. In $S2$, the probabilities that the agents reach, respectively, $g3$ and $g4$ in less than 19 h are, respectively, 0.6 and 0.5. Hence, the joint probability is 0.3. The probabilities that the agents reach their goals are similar in $S3$. In an alternative decomposition, one agent owns the goal rights for 6 h while the other owns them for 4 h. Hence, the first agent should reach the goal in less than 18 h while the second agent in less than 20 h. In $S2$, the probabilities of the two events are, respectively, 0.9 and 0.3 and the joint one is 0.27. These two decompositions show that $CyVar_{sa,sg}^{S2}(100, 24) > 0.5$. In $S3$, the probabilities of the two events are, respectively, 0.3 and 0.6 and their joint probability is less than 0.2. Further decompositions are considered to compute CyVar.

7   Conclusion

CyVar extends the Value At Risk statistics to the risk posed by ICT system under attacks by intelligent, goal oriented agents. These agents escalate their privileges by selecting and implementing a sequence of attacks. Our definition of CyVar uses the security stress, a synthetic measure of ICT robustness.

We approximate this measure through the output of an experiment that applies the Haruspex suite to simulate the agents of interest. To show how CyVar relates to both the robustness of a system and the number and the behavior of the attacking agents, we have presented a case study that applies it to compare three versions of an ICS.

This paper has assumed that the data to compute the CyVar statistics is produced through the Haruspex suite by simulating the attacks against the system. Obviously, CyVar does not depend upon this suite because an assessment can produce the data of interest through distinct tools and alternative approaches.

References

1. Baiardi, F., Coro, F., Tonelli, F., Sgandurra, D.: Automating the assessment of ICT risk. J. Inf. Sec. Appl. **19**(3), 182–193 (2014). doi:10.1016/j.jisa.2014.04.002
2. Baiardi, F., Sgandurra, D.: Assessing ICT risk through a monte carlo method. Environ. Syst. Decis. **33**, 1–14 (2013)
3. Baiardi, F., Corò, F., Tonelli, F., Guidi, L.: Gvscan: scanning networks for global vulnerabilities. In: First International Workshop on Emerging Cyberthreats and Countermeasures, Regensburg, Germany (2013)
4. Baiardi, F., Corò, F., Tonelli, F., Sgandurra, D.: A scenario method to automatically assess ICT risk. In: Processing 2014 Parallel and Distributed, Turin, Italy (2014)
5. Baiardi, F., Tonelli, F., Corò, F., Guidi, L.: QSec: supporting security decisions on an IT infrastructure. In: Luiijf, E., Hartel, P. (eds.) CRITIS 2013. LNCS, vol. 8328, pp. 108–119. Springer, Heidelberg (2013)
6. Kotenko, I., Konovalov, A., Shorov, A.: Agent-based modeling and simulation of botnets and botnet defense. In: Conference on Cyber Conflict, pp. 21–44. CCD COE Publications, Tallinn, Estonia (2010)
7. Barreto, A.B., Hieb, H., Edgar, Y.: Developing a complex simulation environment for evaluating cyber attacks. In: The Interservice/Industry Training, Simulation and Education Conference (I/ITSEC) (2012)
8. Sarraute, C., Richarte, G., Lucángeli Obes, J.: An algorithm to find optimal attack paths in nondeterministic scenarios. In: Proceedings of the 4th ACM Workshop on Security and Artificial Intelligence, AISec 2011, pp. 71–80. ACM, New York, NY, USA (2011)
9. Futoransky, A., Miranda, F., Orlicki, J., Sarraute, C.: Simulating cyber-attacks for fun and profit. In: Proceedings of the 2nd International Conference on Simulation Tools and Techniques, Simutools 2009, pp. 4–149 (2009)
10. Ten, C.-W., Manimaran, G., Liu, C.-C.: Cybersecurity for critical infrastructures: attack and defense modeling. IEEE Trans. Syst. Man Cybern. Part A: Syst. Hum. **40**(4), 853–865 (2010)
11. Baiardi, F., Tonelli, F., Bertolini, A., Bertolotti, R., Guidi, L.: Security stress: evaluating ICT robustness through a monte carlo method. In: Ninth CRITIS Conference on Critical Information Infrastructures Security, Lymassol, Cyprus (2014)
12. Vaughn Jr., R.B., Henning, R., Siraj, A.: Information assurance measures and metrics - state of practice and proposed taxonomy. In: Proceedings of the 36th Annual Hawaii International Conference on System Sciences, p. 10 (2003)

13. Schudel, G., Wood, B.: Adversary work factor as a metric for information assurance. In: Proceedings of the 2000 Workshop on New Security Paradigms, NSPW 2000, pp. 23–30. ACM, New York, NY, USA (2000)
14. Langweg, H.: Framework for malware resistance metrics. In: 2nd ACM Workshop on Quality of Protection, pp. 39–44. ACM, New York, NY, USA (2006)
15. Wang, L., Jajodia, S., Singhal, A., Cheng, P., Noel, S.: K-zero day safety: a network security metric for measuring the risk of unknown vulnerabilities. IEEE Trans. Dependable Sec. Comput. 11(1), 30–44 (2014)
16. Jaquith, A.: Security Metrics: Replacing Fear, Uncertainty, and Doubt
17. Payne, S.C.: A guide to security metrics. SANS Institute (2006)
18. Swanson, M.: Security metrics guide for information technology systems. Technical report, NIST, US Department of Commerce (2003)
19. Sarraute, C.: On exploit quality metrics – and how to use them for automated pentesting. In: Proceedings of 8.8 Computer Security Conference (2011)
20. Pamula, J., Jajodia, S., Ammann, P., Swarup, V.: A weakest-adversary security metric for network configuration security analysis. In: 2nd ACM Workshop on Quality of Protection, pp. 31–38. ACM, New York, NY, USA (2006)
21. Böhme, R.: Security metrics and security investment models. In: Echizen, I., Kunihiro, N., Sasaki, R. (eds.) IWSEC 2010. LNCS, vol. 6434, pp. 10–24. Springer, Heidelberg (2010)
22. Gordon, L.A., Loeb, M.P.: The economics of information security investment. ACM Trans. Inf. Syst. Secur. 5(4), 438–457 (2002). doi:10.1145/581271.581274
23. Kundur, D., Feng, X., Liu, S., Zourntos, T., Butler-Purry, K.L.: Towards a framework for cyber attack impact analysis of the electric smart grid. In: 2010 First IEEE International Conference onSmart Grid Communications (SmartGridComm), pp. 244–249. IEEE (2010)
24. La Corte, A., Scatà, M.: Failure analysis and threats statistic to assess risk and security strategy in a communication system. In: ICSNC 2011, The Sixth International Conference on Systems and Networks Communications, pp. 149–154 (2011)
25. Byres, E., Ginter, A., Lingell, J.: How Stuxnet Spread - A Study of Infection Paths in Best Practice Systems. White Paper. Tofino Report, Abterra Technologies ScadaHacker.com (2011)
26. Langner, R.: Stuxnet: Dissecting a cyberwarfare weapon. Security & Privacy, IEEE 9(3), 49–51 (2011)
27. Nai Fovino, I., Masera, M., Guidi, L., Carpi, G.: An experimental platform for assessing scada vulnerabilities and countermeasures in power plants (2010)

Risk and Development

Development of Device-and Service-Profiles for a Safe and Secure Interconnection of Medical Devices in the Integrated Open OR

Alexander Mildner[1,3(✉)], Armin Janß[2], Jasmin Dell'Anna-Pudlik[2], Paul Merz[2], Martin Leucker[3], and Klaus Radermacher[2]

[1] UniTransferKlinik Lübeck, Lübeck, Germany
a.mildner@unitransferklinik.de
[2] Chair of Medical Engineering, Helmholtz-Institute for Biomedical Engineering, RWTH Aachen University, Aachen, Germany
{janss,dellanna,radermacher}@hia.rwth-aachen.de
[3] Institute for Software Engineering and Programming Languages, University of Lübeck, Lübeck, Germany
leucker@isp.uni-luebeck.de

Abstract. Today's integrated OR systems are closed and proprietary, so that the interconnection of components from third-party vendors is only possible with high time and cost effort. An integrated operating theatre with open interfaces, giving clinical operators the opportunity to choose individual medical devices from different manufacturers, would be advantageous for both hospital operators and small and medium-sized manufacturers of medical devices. Actual standards and concepts regarding technical feasibility and accreditation process do not cope with the requirements for modular integration based on an open standard. Therefore, strategies as well as device-and service-profiles to enable a procedure for risk management and certification capability are in the focus of the BMBF-funded OR.NET-project. The use of standardized device-and service-profiles shall allow the manufacturers to integrate their medical devices without disclosing the medical devices' risk analysis and related confidential expertise or proprietary information.

Keywords: Accreditation strategies · Medical device integration · Dynamic interconnection · Open standards · Interoperability · OR.net project · Risk management · Usability engineering · Device-and service-profiles

1 Introduction and Background

1.1 Current Situation

The need for integration and interoperability of medical devices in the operating room (OR) and clinical environment is growing. The reason for this is, inter alia, the increasingly complex surgical equipment: the surgeons, anesthetists and OR nurses often work highly cramped and stressed and have to deal with the operation of many different complex and mostly complete independently working medical devices, which in general are incompatible.

© Springer International Publishing Switzerland 2015
F. Seehusen et al. (Eds.): RISK 2015, LNCS 9488, pp. 65–74, 2015.
DOI: 10.1007/978-3-319-26416-5_5

This can be solved e.g. by using an integrated workflow-adapted surgical and anesthetic cockpit, for which an interconnection of devices has to be possible. Today, this is only feasible by using isolated proprietary solutions from a single manufacturer. In this case, because there are no open standards for the interconnection of devices and the exchange of data between medical devices, the use of proprietary interfaces inhibits the general interchangeability of medical devices.

Today's proprietary interconnection of medical devices is based on company-specific interfaces - however no common standards for the interconnection and exchange of data from medical devices, both among each other and to the adjacent (Medical-) IT-Systems exist. Third-party vendors in most cases are not able to participate in the proprietary solution.

1.2 Goal

Therefore, the goal is the creation of an open standard, which allows an open and dynamic interconnection and integration of medical devices. This standardized, open and dynamic interconnection of medical devices is on the one hand a technical challenge and on the other hand a legitimate barrier. According to actual medical device directive 93/42 EEC the hospital operator faces the trouble to become the producer/manufacturer of an open integrated OR system. Therefore, system manufacturer obligations concerning declaration of conformity should not be transferred to the operator, in order to keep the accreditation process practicable.

Such interconnection would be advantageous for both hospital operators and small and medium-sized manufacturers of medical devices. The hospital operators would be able to modularly and flexibly combine medical devices, which provide the optimal support for the specific diagnosis and therapy procedures. Operation workflows and clinical processes could be conducted in a more effective and efficient way. The clinical staff would be relieved by an improved usability of the integrated devices system compared to single devices and patient safety would be increased. Small and medium-sized manufacturers of medical devices would be able to participate in integrated ORs.

The OR.NET-project, funded by the Federal Ministry of Education and Research (BMBF), focuses on the safe, secure and dynamic interconnection of medical devices in the operating room and clinic on the basis of open standards [1]. The project includes almost 80 project partners ranging from medical device manufacturers, clinic operators, and standardization organizations up to research institutes. Main goals in the OR.NET project on one hand is the standardized technical solution for the interoperability of medical devices and on the other hand the possibility for clinical operators to choose and interconnect medical devices without the effort of additional accreditation process and legal responsibility for the resulting system.

1.3 Strategy

The aim must be a standardardized open interface for the dynamic interconnection of medical devices with documented technical and HMI specifications and requirements. In the documentation of the interface the protocol specification has to be addressed, which however is not sufficient in the medical field due to regulatory requirements and necessary risk considerations. Rather also a documentation of the boundary conditions, requirements on the infrastructure and on the other side of the interface (the connected medical device(s)) must be available.

To establish a safe, open interconnection, these must be planned already in the development of a medical device. The necessary information shall be documented with the help of a device-and service-profile. This device-and service-profile would serve manufacturers to generically document information regarding the interface of the medical device and to provide information for potential network partners (medical devices) and the operator.

So far, an extended device-and service-profile has been developed in the framework of the OR.NET project and is currently being evaluated. The extended technical device profile contains inter alia additional information regarding the extended intended use, network communication risks (manufacturers' responsibility) and network requirements (clinical operators' responsibility) as well as User Interface Descriptions. The extended medical device and service profile complements the standardization activities in the OR.NET project e.g. regarding the ISO 11073 extensions for the data model and especially for safety aspects of medical device communications.

2   State-of-the-Art

Today's concept of proprietarily interconnected medical devices follows the principle that the connection of two medical devices implies the creation of a medical device system, which regulatorily counts as a new medical device [4]. In this case, one of the medical device manufacturers acts as a system producer and assumes the responsibility for the joint operation of the medical devices, declares conformity with the directive(s) and yet ensures the necessary requirements of risk management and usability assessment [2].

To meet the market demands, several medical technology companies offer integrated operating systems based on proprietary interfaces. For example, the OR1 system by Karl Storz is a fully integrated operating room for minimal-invasive surgery with an interface for the connection to hospital information systems and telemedicine communication. Furthermore e.g. Brainlab, Stryker, Maquet and Olympus offer integrated OR solutions. All those OR-systems can be controlled centrally via a touch screen or partially a voice control. The systems are based on proprietary interfaces, which only allow a combination of specific medical devices where other medical device manufacturers are not able to participate. If a manufacturer wants to cooperate in one of the existing integrated OR-systems, he has to adapt his medical device to the OR-producers' proprietary protocol specifications. This means much time and cost effort and the manufacturer is not able to put his integrated device on the market himself. In consequence, for small and medium-sized medical device manufacturers it is difficult and elaborate to play a role in existing OR-systems [1].

The actual accreditation process does not fit to the vision of dynamically interconnected open systems in Medical-IT-Networks. The integration of individual medical units by the operator would actually imply (according to medical device law) an in-house production regarding the integrated work system. The operator is not and will not be able as well as unwilling to assume obligations (further human resources, conducting accreditation process…) of a medical device manufacturer.

Regarding this, the situation forces clinic operators either to restrict themselves to the proprietary solution of one medical device manufacturer or to use stand-alone medical devices. In the first case, it is not possible to combine the best-fitting medical devices for the specific purpose (best of breed strategy); in the second case, the benefits of an integrated and networked operation environment cannot be exploited.

3   Approach

Because the dynamic interconnection has significant benefits for medical application scenarios and state-of-the-art methods for the accreditation process are insufficient, a new approach for the conformity declaration and (technical and HMI-based) risk management has to be drawn up. First and foremost this includes methodological determination of new requirements and risks resulting from the ability of open integrated medical devices.

Network-based risks as well as requirements concerning unknown network partners have to be documented in a standardized way. Our approach defines a device-and service-profile, which includes all necessary information for a safe and reliable interconnection. The profile can be used by manufacturers of medical devices during the product development process to document the interface specifications and requirements for the OR-infrastructure and connected devices.

The EN 80001-1 [3] defines requirements regarding network-characteristics, which the medical device manufacturer has to communicate to the hospital operator. These are refined in EN 60601-1 [4] and define a basis of information the device-and service-profile should contain:

- The purpose of the medical device's connection to an IT-Network, how the integrated system is intended to be used;
- The required characteristics/performance for the IT-Network incorporating the medical device;
- The required configuration of the IT-Network incorporating the medical device;
- The intended information flow between the medical device, the Medical-IT-Network and other medical devices on the medical IT-Network and, if relevant to the key properties, the intended routing through the Medical-IT-Network;
- The constraints on the extendibility of the system IT-Network;
- The specifications of all Medical Electrical Equipment and other equipment to be integrated;
- The performance of each Medical Electrical Equipment and other equipment.

When putting medical devices into service in an open network, the hospital operator compares the device-and service-profiles to verify the safe interconnection and communication of specific device pairings. This verification is performed in the form of a Delta-analysis of two device profiles, as shown in Fig. 1.

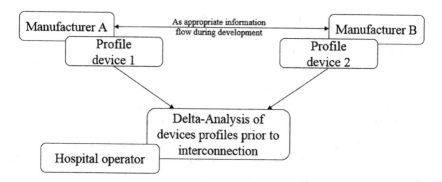

Fig. 1. Delta-analysis for open integration

The device-and service-profile should address five topics of concern, which are derived in the following subchapters.

3.1 Intended Use and Corresponding Risk Analysis

According to Directive 93/42/EEC for medical devices, an intended use has to be defined, documented and publicized by the manufacturer. This intended use documents the medical purpose and function of a medical device.

When interconnecting medical devices in a network, it turns out that in most cases this (medical) intended use of the original medical device to be cross-linked is not affected. Thus arises, for example, in interconnecting a surgical microscope system and a surgical cutting instrument with regard to sharing of input and output devices of the microscope system (foot switch, manual switches, display of setting parameters) that the respective medical intended uses of the devices are not changed by interconnection [2].

Neither the main functions of the medical devices, derived from the intended use, are changed. The network consists merely in other technical realization of functions: instead of using the foot switch of the cutting device, an integrated foot switch (which fulfils the safety requirements regarding technical and HMI-based risks) for controlling a cutting device is used, so only one input device is replaced by another.

For the benefit due to interconnecting medical devices, the (technical) intended use of the interconnection must be documented, which is considered to be an extension of the original intended use of the device. This extension includes the intended use of the service or the device in the cross-linked system with other interconnectable services or devices and the type of data exchange.

To provide interconnection of medical devices with unknown manufacturers, it may be convenient to define groups or classes of medical devices (like cutting devices, central Workstations, etc.) and define client and server of an interconnection. At this point, for interconnections with special needs, a whitelist of devices allowed for interconnection could be documented.

In order to control one medical device function by another medical device, the documentation of the development process as well as the software of the influencing device must, if applicable, be adjusted to the requirements of the risk class of the influenced medical device. Thereby the medical device manufacturer may have to meet additional requirements as part of the approval process.

The nature of influence structured ascending according to risk potential as follows:

- Read: Visualization/information purposes (no change)
- Write: use influence (if appropriate adjustment of the risk class)
- Read/Write: control (if appropriate adjustment of the risk class)

As an example a connection of a central user-interface with a cutting device: For data transfer from cutting device to a central user-interface for visualization or data acquisition for documentation purposes no adjustment of the documentation regarding regulatory requirements of the risk class of the central user-interface is required. For changing parameters or controlling triggering condition of the cutting device through the central user interface or one of its components (application control) the regulatory requirements of the risk class of the controlled cutting device have to be met. If appropriate, for future influencing devices, a simplified modular-development-documentation can be achieved, in which only modules involved in cross-linking are affected by the regulatory requirements of the risk class of the affected device.

In addition, a separate conformity statement of control elements, such as a universal footswitch that controls both devices, is possible.

According to the standard DIN EN ISO 14971: "Application of risk management to medical devices" [5], for every medical device and system of medical devices a risk analysis regarding patient or user harm, which is based on the intended use and functions of the medical device, has to be performed. Residual risks derived from the risk analysis must be weighted against the clinical benefits. Risk mitigation measures must be specified individually by the manufacturer or can be taken out of standards like EN 60601-1 (where several hazards and risk measures for medical electrical equipment are listed). This risk analysis has to be checked for delta changes when cross-linking medical devices. If there are changes on the medical intended use and the necessary functions to meet this intended use, this has to be included in the medical risk analysis.

3.2 Technical Description of Interface

When interconnecting medical devices, a comparison of the specifications of the components used to implement the functions and the protocol specification has to be assured. Only when mutually the specification requirements are met, devices may be connected.

An interconnection of medical devices over a hospital IT-Network is necessarily based on a network-technology (in the project OR.NET on Ethernet), so that it is possible to describe the technical specifications regarding transmission in a structured interface description. Thus, if it mutually can be ensured, that the communication transmitted and received according to the interface description, a safe networking capability can be assumed.

The definition and standardization of the technical interface specification is another focus of the OR.NET-project. The technical interface description is based on the IEEE 11073 medical device communication standard and currently has the status draft:

The draft consist firstly of general device information, such as data model version, which is implemented in the device, and devices information of the MDS (Medical Device System) descriptor (e.g. model-no, model name, serial No, manufacturer, friendly name, UDI). Secondly, the medical device has to be described technically, as described in the data model, which dissects a medical device system (MDS) into subparts to metrics (such as a single parameter, value,…). This approach is directly in line to the function tree FMEA, so that a direct risk analysis after FMEA methodology can be applied. Any function that represents the device and is available via the interface is described in detail. The description includes inter alia:

- Range: If present, the value range of the parameter/date is set. It may be that can be defined a specific range of values
- The type of communication: What kind of message/information transfer is expected to: periodically (consignment within a defined time interval), episodic (shipment value/status change), polling (sink retrieves values, if needed), stream
- Settability (Read/Write): Specifies whether a value can only be read or written (if settable: relative, absolute, presets)

Thus, the technical specifications provide a model of the medical device and describe the medical device as presented in the network.

3.3 User Interface Profiles

UI-Profiles allow the manufacturers to integrate their medical devices, respectively the provided functions regarding HMI requirements, into the OR.NET network. The UI-Profiles allow both an automated optimized selection and composition of various user interfaces and implicitly an optimal design of a central GUI with respect to the criteria of usability and an integrated human risk analysis [6]. The core of the UI-Profiles are attributes (characteristics of input and output devices as well as GUI interaction elements, human information processing factors, environmental and process factors, task-specific factors, criticality of device functions, grouping of interaction elements, requirements for input and output devices, etc.) and the dependencies of the attributes, which are described in four matrices [7]: generation/selection of interaction element and input device, visual presentation of information, acoustic information presentation and visual grouping.

Based on these matrices an integrated user interface can be evaluated and furthermore designed. The UI-Profiles are defined as additional information in the technical device-profile (including identification, type, subtype, functions, manufacturer, etc.). With the help of a systematic modelling and human risk analysis technique, the way for standardized GUI development of integrated medical devices shall be paved.

3.4 Technical Risk Management

In medical device and software development, risk management is obligatory. Besides that, since in most cases the medical intended use and the "medical risk analysis" do not or only marginally change, when making a medical device interoperable it is reasonable to also perform a technical risk analysis regarding two domains:

1. Hazards concerning changed parts, components and software modules of a medical device: Hazards, which occur during the development of an interconnectable medical product, however, on the one hand lead to infrastructure requirements and on the other hand lead to device-internal security measures.

   Infrastructure requirements have to be documented in the device-and service-profile as network requirements.

   Internal security measures have to be implemented during the development process of the medical device and should be completed when declaring conformity. Due to the internal nature of the security measures, they must be communicated in exceptional cases when they produce requirements to the application level of the communication partner, which cannot be mutually intercepted on the communication protocol level.

   The risk management standard EN ISO 14971 helps the medical device manufacturer with lists of hazards and possible causes to look for while developing a medical device, but does not give network-specific input for risk analysis.

   The DIN EN 60601-1 (a standard for the development of electrical medical devices) addresses in annex H.7.2 this subject with some points for "causes of HAZARDOUS SITUATIONS associated with IT-NETWORKS". These follow the same idea as hazards for changed parts/components and software modules interconnected medical devices.

2. Hazards concerning the interconnection and communication over an IT-Network: When integrating medical devices over a Medical-IT-Network, hazards arising from the interconnection have to be considered. In general, devices are not exclusively connected directly and bilaterally. In the Medical-IT-Network are also other medical and non-medical devices and possibly various infrastructure components involved in the communication. Through influences occurring from those network-components, various error possibilities on the transmission path between the communication partners arise. For this reason, security measures have to be defined which allow, if necessary, the inference of a message transmission and receipt. These security measures must be communicated between the network partners, as they are only useful if both sides meet them or at least the recipient of a message can handle the safety measure. Therefore, it is useful to present these measures in the device-and service-profile.

   The profile is also available for the hospital operator, who is responsible for establishing the interconnection. The compliance of the safety measures has to be checked prior to establishment of this interconnection; only with positive outcome in the pre-tests, the interconnection is verified and legal. The interconnection of medical devices over an Medical-IT-Network is considered in some standards, like the EN 60601-1, which in annex H.7.2 addresses "Causes of HAZARDOUS SITUATIONS associated with IT-NETWORKS": loss of data, inappropriate data interchange, corrupted data, inappropriate timing of data, unexpected receipt of data and unauthorized access to data. In addition, the EN 61784-3-1 references on network-caused communication faults and defines security measures. According to these standards and regarding the protocol and data model of OR.NET, a list of communication based security measures have been defined: sequence number, time stamp, encryption, authorization via certificate, response, 2-channel-transmission, safety-context and periodic data transfer. These security measures can be used stand-alone or combined, regarding the type of data, which is transferred. According to EN 80001-1, possible hazardous situations concerning a network failure have to be documented to be analyzed by the hospital operator when interconnecting medical devices the first time.

So the medical device manufacturer has to publish a small part of the risk analysis regarding hazards to the three key properties, which can arise of a network failure (safety, effectiveness, data and systems security).

3.5 Network Requirements

From the technical risk analysis of "Hazards concerning changed parts, components and software modules of a medical device" and "Hazards concerning the interconnection of medical devices and communication over an IT-network" several requirements to the network are arising, which have to be documented and to be fulfilled for the correct and secure operation of the interconnected medical devices. The hospital operator, which usually is in charge of the network, has to ensure that these requirements are met. The EN 60601-1 and the EN 80001-1 address some of those requirements and are amended by Quality-of-Service (QoS)-aspects: Maximum acceptable response time, acceptable failure rate of the network, availability of the network (planned and unplanned maintenance), normal network loads/bandwidth, peak network load, jitter, packet loss rate, the required configuration of the IT-Network incorporating the medical device and network management meeting requirements of EN 80001.

Since the operator must be aware of these requirements, they must be listed in the device-and service-profile. Only if the operator is able to provide the necessary network infrastructure in accordance with the fulfilment of the requirements of the medical devices, a secure interconnection can be guaranteed.

4 Conclusion and Future Work

In this paper, accreditation aspects in the development process of open networked medical devices have been considered. The responsibilities for the development, production, operation and decommissioning as well as the conformity statement of open integrated medical devices have been addressed and the need of defined and standardized device-and service-profiles have been derived.

Risk assessment possibilities have been developed for open medical work systems and differentiated between hazards concerning changed parts, components and software modules of a medical device and hazards concerning the interconnection of medical devices and communication over an IT-network.

Consequently, hazards concerning changed parts, components and software modules of a medical device must be secured by the manufacturers' internal risk measures similar to today's medical device development process, hazards concerning the interconnection of medical devices and communication over an IT-network must be communicated in the device-and service-profiles. Examples of infrastructure requirements have been defined, which have to be fulfilled by the hospital operator for a safe and secure integration.

For interoperable medical devices a structured and standardized interface description of the capabilities and requirements is essential. A documentation in form of device-and service-profiles seems reasonable to meet this requirement.

Furthermore, it will be necessary to elaborate device-and service-profiles regarding the creation of device classes and security levels. The process of accreditation documentation regarding the delta of the device-and service-profiles has to be produced exemplarily for different device combinations. Specific device-interconnections and clinical scenarios (use cases) should support this elaboration in order to identify weaknesses and lack of information and to complete the risk aspects described in this paper. Finally, all developed information and procedures regarding the device-and service-profiles (including UI-Profiles) should be formally described for incorporation in a software supported process model in order to achieve automatic use.

References

1. Birkle, M., Benzko, J., Shevchenko, N.: Das Projekt OR.NET - Sichere dynamische Vernetzung in OP und Klinik. Deutsche Zeitschrift für klinische Forschung, Innovation und. Praxis **11**(12), 41–45 (2012)
2. Kuehn, F., Leucker, M., Mildner, A.: OR.NET - approaches for risk analysis and measures of dynamically interconnected medical devices. In: 5th Workshop on Medical Cyber-Physical Systems: OASIcs, vol. 36, pp. 133–136. Schloss Dagstuhl-Leibniz-Zentrum fuer Informatik (2014)
3. DIN EN 80001–1:2011-11, VDE 0756-1:2011-11: Application of risk management for IT-networks incorporating medical devices - Part 1: roles, responsibilities and activities (IEC 80001-1:2010), German version EN 80001-1:2011 (2011)
4. DIN EN 60601–1:2013-12, VDE 0750-1:2013-12: Medical electrical equipment - Part 1: general requirements for basic safety and essential performance (IEC 60601-1:2005 + Cor.: 2006 + Cor.:2007 + A1:2012), German version EN 60601-1:2006 + Cor.:2010 + A1:2013 (2013)
5. DIN EN ISO 14971: Medical devices - application of risk management to medical devices (ISO 14971:2007, Corrected version 2007–10-01), German version EN ISO 14971:2012 (2012)
6. Benzko, J., Janß, A., Dell'Anna, J., Radermacher, K.: Man-machine interfaces in the operating room. In: Proceedings of the 48th DGBMT Annual Conference, vol. 59, p. 430 (2014)
7. Janß, A., Benzko, J., Merz, P., Dell'Anna, J., Strake, M., Radermacher, K.: Development of medical device UI-profiles for reliable and safe human-machine-interaction in the integrated operating room of the future. In: Proceedings of the 5th International Conference on Applied Human Factors and Ergonomics 2014, pp. 1855–1860 (2014)

Security Testing

Using CAPEC for Risk-Based Security Testing

Fredrik Seehusen[✉]

Department for Networked Systems and Services, SINTEF ICT,
Blindern, PO Box 124, 0314 Oslo, Norway
fredrik.seehusen@sintef.no

Abstract. We present a method for risk-based security testing that takes a set of CAPEC attack patterns as input and produces a risk model which can be used for security test identification and prioritization. Since parts of the method can be automated, we believe that the method will speed up the process of constructing a risk model significantly. We also argue that the constructed risk model is suitable for security test identification and prioritization.

Keywords: Risk assessment · Testing · Security · Risk-based testing

1 Introduction

Risk assessment and testing are two areas that are traditionally addressed in isolation and that are supported by dedicated tools and processes, e.g. ISO31000 [1] for risk assessment and ISO/IEEE 29119 [2] for testing. However, the combination of these two areas can be mutually benefiting. On the one hand, the risk assessment can be used to guide the testing. On the other hand, the testing can be used to validate the risk model estimates.

A risk-based testing process is a process obtained by adding a structured risk assessment activity to a traditional testing process. In order for this enhanced process to be an improvement over the traditional testing process, the time spent on the added risk activity must make up for the loss of time spent on the traditional testing activities. It is therefore desirable that the risk assessment should not be too time consuming and it should result in a risk picture which is useful for the testing.

In this paper, we present a method and a technique which addresses both of these issues. Firstly, the method automates much of the process of constructing a risk model, and also the process of test-identification and prioritization based on risk models. Secondly, the method produces risk models that describe CAPEC attack patterns including known vulnerabilities which provide a relevant starting point for security test identification.

The expected end user of our method is a security tester and/or a risk analyst. From the user perspective, the method has three steps. In Step I, the user selects a set of attack patterns from the CAPEC dictionary of attack patterns [9] and generates a risk model automatically using our CAPEC to risk model technique.

© Springer International Publishing Switzerland 2015
F. Seehusen et al. (Eds.): RISK 2015, LNCS 9488, pp. 77–92, 2015.
DOI: 10.1007/978-3-319-26416-5_6

In step II of the method, the user manually refines the risk model in order to make it system/domain specific. In Step III, the user automatically generates a prioritized list of test procedures from the risk model using our technique test procedure prioritization. The resulting test procedures are intended to be used as starting point for test design, implementation, and execution.

The main contribution of this paper is the description of the method and the technique for automated risk model generation based on CAPEC attack patterns. The technique for test procedure derivation and prioritization is described in a separate paper [14]. There are many approaches to risk-based testing, but we are not aware of any approaches that automates the construction of a risk model which is used for test identification and prioritization.

The paper is structured as follows: In Sect. 2 we provide an overview of our method and describe the criteria it is intended to fulfill. In Sects. 3, 4, and 5 we respectively describe step I, step II, and step III of our method in more detail. In Sect. 6 we discuss related work and in Sect. 7 we provide conclusions.

2   Overview of Method and Success Criteria

In this section, we give and overview our method for using CAPEC attack patterns in a risk-based testing process and describe criteria it is intended to fulfill. In general, it is not given that any combination of risk assessment and testing is useful. There are many risk assessment methods. These differ w.r.t. to the way in which the risk assessment is documented, the degree of structure, and the intended target time. For instance, some check list based approaches may only take a few hours while other more rigorous approaches may take thousands of hours. In any case, in a risk-based testing process, the time spent on the risk assessment should make up for the time lost in the testing activity. Therefore it is important the risk assessment is not too time consuming.

In addition to this, the outcome of the risk assessment, which we will refer to as a *risk model*, should provide useful input to the testing activity in the sense that it will reduce time and/or increase quality of the test results. There are many different kinds of risk model documentation languages, and not all of them may be suitable. Furthermore, the risk model has to be on the right level of abstraction and have the right focus. For instance, if it is too vague or documents risks and circumstances that cannot be investigated through testing, then the risk model might not be suitable.

In summary, we believe that the fulfillment of the following criteria will increase the likelihood of a risk-based testing process being an improvement over a traditional testing process:

C1 The risk assessment should not be too time consuming.
C2 The risk assessment should help reduce the time spent on test identification/design.
C3 The risk assessment should help increase the quality of the testing activity.

The method presented in this paper is supported by two techniques/transformations (both of which have been implemented in proof-of-concept tools) which help automate parts of the process:

T1 A transformation from CAPEC attack a patterns into CORAS risk models.
T2 A transformation from CORAS risk models into a prioritized list of test
  procedures.

Fig. 1. Method overview

As illustrated in Fig. 1, the method has three steps. In step I, the users
selects a set of attack pattern from the CAPEC dictionary, and then uses **T1**
to automatically generate a CORAS risk model. In step II, the user refines the
resulting risk model to make it specific to the target of analysis. This step has
to be performed manually. In Sect. 4, we will discuss different ways in which the
risk model can be refined. In step III, the users annotates the risk model with
test specific annotations, and uses **T2** to automatically generate a prioritized
list of test procedures which can be used as starting point for test design.

The two techniques and the three steps of the method are meant to be used
a part of a more comprehensive process for risk assessment and security testing.
To illustrate this, we have in Fig. 2 mapped the three steps of the method (as
shown by the labeled circles) onto typical activities of a risk assessment and
a testing process, in this case, corresponding to ISO31000 [1], and ISO/IEEE
29119 [2], respectively.

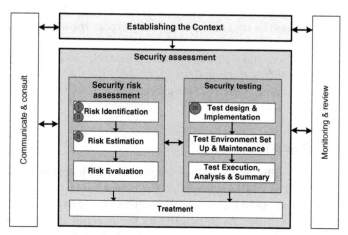

Fig. 2. Method context

3 Step I: From CAPEC to Generic CORAS Risk Models

In step I of our method, the user selects a set of attack patterns from the CAPEC
dictionary and uses **T1** to automatically generate a CORAS risk model.

As shown in Fig. 2, we assume that an *Establishing the Context* activity is performed before entering into step I. We will not describe this activity in detail since it is not specific to the method we present. However, typical artefacts that may have been described before entering into step I are: the target of evaluation; likelihood and consequence scale definitions; asset definitions; risk evaluation criteria.

For selecting the relevant CAPEC attack patterns, the user should formulate clear attack pattern selection criteria, and then walk through the list of all attack patterns and discard those patterns which do not fulfill the critera. Examples of possible critera are:

– The attack pattern must be within the scope of the system under evaluation. For instance, if the attack pattern describes how to exploit a particular functionality such as login, and the target system does not have that functionality, the attack pattern would not satisfy the criterion.
– The attack pattern must exploit a weakness which is on the CWE (Common Weakness Enumeration) [10] list of top 25 most severe weaknesses.

The selection of the CAPEC attack patterns should be supported by a tool which allows the user to browse the attack patterns, and mark those which will be used as a basis for risk model generation. We have a developed a proof-of-concept tool for doing this. The tool allows the user to import the CAPEC dictionary (represented as an XML file), and display its contents in a tree view showing only information which is relevant for the translation into CORAS risk models. The tree view allows the user to delete and edit attack patterns, as well as to supply addition parameters to the transformation. After this editing is done, the user may use the tool to automatically export the attack patterns into a CORAS risk model.

In the following, we make precise what we mean by a *CORAS risk model* (Sect. 3.1) and a *CAPEC attack pattern* (Sect. 3.2), then we describe the technique **T1** for translating CAPEC attack patterns to CORAS risk models (Sect. 3.3).

3.1 CORAS Risk Models

There are many different kinds of languages for describing risk models. Our technique uses the CORAS language for model-based risk assessment [8]. CORAS risk models are used for documenting risks as well as events and circumstances that can cause risks. As illustrated by the example in Fig. 3, a CORAS risk model is a directed acyclic graph where every node is of one of the following kinds:

Threat. A potential cause of an unwanted incident or threat scenario.
Threat scenario. A chain or series of events that is initiated by a threat and that may lead to an unwanted incident.
Unwanted incident. An event that harms or reduces the value of an asset.

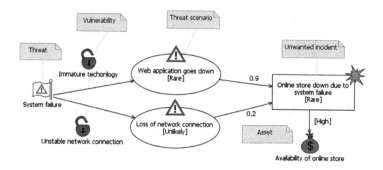

Fig. 3. Example of a CORAS risk model

Asset. Something to which a party assigns value and hence for which the party requires protection.

Note that risks can also be represented in a CORAS risk model. These correspond to pairs of unwanted incidents and assets. If an unwanted incident harms exactly one asset, as is the case in Fig. 3, then this unwanted incident will represent a single risk.

Relations and nodes may have the following assignments:

Likelihood values may be assigned to a threat scenario and unwanted incident A, estimating the likelihood of A occurring.

Conditional likelihood values may be assigned to relations going from A to B, estimating the conditional likelihood that B occurs given that A has occurred.

Consequence values may be assigned to relations going from A to B, estimating the consequence the occurrence of A has on B.

Vulnerabilities may be assigned to relations going from A to B, describing a weakness, flaw or deficiency that opens for A leading to B.

3.2 Common Attack Pattern Enumeration and Classification (CAPEC)

CAPEC is a comprehensive dictionary and classification taxonomy of known security attacks [9]. It contains more than 400 attack patterns, all of which are described in terms of a set of *attributes* such as attack name, method of attack, related weaknesses, typical severity etc. In order to define a transformation from a CAPEC attack pattern to a CORAS risk model, we must ask

– What attributes of an attack can be expressed in a CORAS risk model?
– Which of these attributes are described by the CAPEC attack pattern?

In answer to the first question, we believe that the following information about a security attack can be represented and would be of value in a CORAS risk model:

A The name of the attack.

B An estimate of how likely it is that the attack is initiated.

C An estimate of how likely it is that the attack will succeed given that it is initiated.

D A list of consequences/unwanted incidents which a successful attack can cause/lead to.

E An estimate of how likely it is that a successful attack will lead to the unwanted incidents.

F A list of assets that can be affected by the unwanted incidents of successful attacks.

G A description of which assets that can be harmed by an unwanted incident.

H An estimate of the consequence that an unwanted incident has on each of its assets.

I A list of vulnerabilities that can be exploited by the attack.

The attributes which can be derived from a CAPEC attack pattern are A, C, D, F, G, H, and I. Information about the attributes which are not described by a CAPEC attack pattern (B and E) can be supplied as input to the transformation to the risk model or/and as part of step II of our method.

Table 1 shows the format of the CAPEC attributes which can be expressed in a CORAS risk model. Henceforth, whenever we write CAPEC attack pattern, or attack pattern, we will mean an instance of the Table 1. Note that a CAPEC attack pattern may include many more attributes than those shown in Table 1. However, these attributes are difficult to expressed in a CORAS risk model, and are therefore ignored by our translation.

In Tables 2 and 3, we have given examples of CAPEC attack pattern 34 and 64, respectively.

Table 1. Format of a CAPEC attack pattern

Name	A pair (ID, N) where ID denotes the identifier of the attack pattern and N denotes the name of the pattern
Typical likelihood of exploit	A likelihood LE denoting the likelihood that the attack will succeed
Attack motivation-consequences	A list $(TI_1, S_1), (TI_2, S_2), \dots (TI_n, S_n)$ of n pairs of the form (TI, S), where TI denotes the name of a technical impact and S denotes the scope of TI given as a subset of the set {Availability, Confidentiality, Integrity}
CIA impact	A triple (cia_c, cia_i, cia_a) denoting the impact/consequence the attack has on confidentiality, integrity, and availability, respectively
CWE ID (Related weaknesses)	A list $v_1, v_2, \dots, v_n$ of n elements denoting CWE vulnerabilities that can be exploited by the attack

Table 2. Example of CAPEC attack pattern 34

Name	(CAPEC-34, HTTP Response Splitting)
Typical likelihood of exploit	Medium
Attack motivation-consequences	(Execute unauthorized code or commands, Confidentiality, Integrity, Availability), (Gain privileges / assume identify, Confidentiality)
CIA impact	(High, High, Low)
CWE ID (Related weaknesses)	CWE-113 Improper Neutralization of CRLF Sequences in HTTP Headers ('HTTP Response Splitting'), CWE-697 Insufficient Comparison, CWE-707 Improper Enforcement of Message or Data Structure, CWE-713 OWASP Top Ten 2007 Category A2 - Injection Flaws

Table 3. Example of CAPEC attack pattern 62

Name	(CAPEC-62,Cross Site Request Forgery (aka Session Riding))
Typical likelihood of exploit	High
Attack motivation-consequences	(Read application data, Confidentiality), (Modify application data, Integrity), (Gain privileges / assume identity, Confidentiality)
CIA impact	(High, High, Low)
CWE ID (Related weaknesses)	CWE-352 Cross-Site Request Forgery (CSRF), CWE-664 Improper Control of a Resource Through its Lifetime, CWE-732 Incorrect Permission Assignment for Critical Resource, CWE-716 OWASP Top Ten 2007 Category A5 - Cross Site Request Forgery (CSRF)

3.3 From CAPEC Instances to Generic CORAS Risk Models

Having made precise what is meant by a CORAS risk model and a CAPEC attack pattern we now describe the translation from a set of attack patterns to a CORAS risk model.

The information which cannot be derived from a CAPEC pattern can be supplied to the transformation in addition to the CAPEC instances. In particular, this information is:

- a mapping lm from CAPEC likelihoods to CORAS likelihoods;
- a default initiation likelihood dil, specifying the likelihood that an attack will be initiated;
- a default technical impact likelihood $dtil$ specifying the conditional likelihood of a successful attack leading to a technical impact.

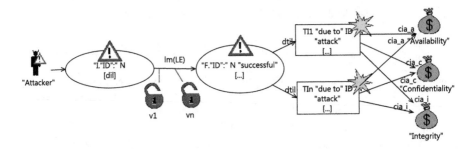

Fig. 4. CORAS risk model showing outcome of translation function

Given this information, the outcome of a transformation from a CAPEC instance on the form shown in Table 1 will in the general case be a CORAS risk model on the form shown in Fig. 4. To distinguish between variables and strings/constants, we have in Fig. 4 denoted all non-variables inside quotation marks. For instance, we have written "Attacker", meaning that Attacker is not a variable, but should appear as a constant string which is not dependent on the CAPEC instance being translated. The variables in the diagram such as ID, N, v_1, LE, etc. are all taken from the CAPEC instance which is assumed to be the input to the translation (see Table 1).

As illustrated in Fig. 4, each CAPEC instance is translated into two threat scenarios: one threat scenario corresponding to the initiation of the attack, and one threat scenario corresponding to a successful attack. The threat scenario describing attack initiation is given likelihood dil. The condition likelihood that the attack will be successful given that it is initiated is given by $lm(LE)$, i.e. the exploit likelihood of the CAPEC instance LE translated to the CORAS model likelihood by function lm.

Given that the attack described by the CAPEC instance is successful, it can lead to one or more technical impacts with conditional likelihood $dtil$. Each technical impact of the CAPEC instance is translated to an unwanted incident in the CORAS model. These unwanted incidents may in turn be connected to one of the three assets Availability, Confidentiality, or Integrity, and the consequences of the unwanted incidents towards these is given by the CIA values of the CAPEC instance.

The assets that a technical impact is connected to are decided by the scope of the technical impact. For instance, if the scope of the technical impact includes all three assets, then the technical impact will be connected to all the three assets. If the scope only includes e.g. Confidentiality, then the technical impact will only be connected to the Confidentiality asset.

Each weakness of the CAPEC attack pattern is translated to a vulnerability in the CORAS risk model (shown as a red lock) and attached to the relation going from the threat scenario describing attack initiation to the threat scenario describing attack success.

As an example, assume that we supply the following input to the translation: the CAPEC instances 34 and 62 shown in Tables 2 and 3, respectively; a mapping lm defined by $\{Low \mapsto eLow, Medium \mapsto eMedium, High \mapsto eHigh\}$; a default initiation likelihood $iHigh$; a default technical impact likelihood $tMedium$. Then the output of the translation will be the CORAS risk model shown in Fig. 5. Note that the likelihood values of the threat scenarios describing successful attacks and unwanted incidents describing attack consequences are undefined. However, these likelihood values can be calculated automatically from the other likelihood values in the risk model as described in e.g. [8] or [14].

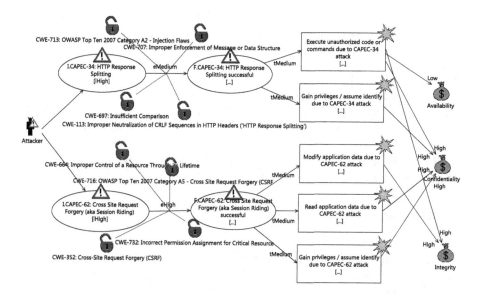

Fig. 5. Risk model obtained by translation of CAPEC-34 and CAPEC-62

4   Step II: From Generic CORAS Risk Models to Target Specific Risk Models

The translation of CAPEC instances results in a CORAS risk model which is not specific to a particular system under test or target of evaluation. For this reason, we suggest that CORAS risk model be manually refined to make it more relevant for a particular target of evaluation. There are several different ways that the CORAS risk model can be refined for this purpose. In this section, we cover the most important ones.

4.1   Refinement of Likelihood and Consequence Values

All likelihood and consequences of the CORAS risk model obtained from a set of CAPEC instances are not specific to the target of evaluation. One way of refining the risk model is therefore to examine each likelihood and consequence estimate of the risk model, and adjust them as necessary. For instance, both threat scenarios describing attack initiation are in Fig. 5 given the likelihood *iHigh*. As previously described, this a default likelihood value which is supplied as an additional parameter to the transformation since the likelihood cannot be derived from the CAPEC patterns. The user of our approach should examine these likelihood values in particular, and adjust them if necessary.

4.2   Refinement by Element Splitting

In some cases, it may be the case that some of the attacks or technical impacts derived from the CAPEC instances are described in a too generic way. In these cases, the user should consider refining the risk model by splitting threat scenarios or unwanted incidents. For instance, if it necessary to distinguish between different features of the target of evaluation that are subject to the attack, then this can expressed in the risk model by splitting threat scenarios. For instance, we could split the threat scenario *I. CAPEC-34: HTTP response splitting* in Fig. 5 into the two threat scenarios *I. CAPEC-34A: HTTP response splitting targeting feature A* and *I. CAPEC-34B: HTTP response splitting targeting feature B*. This will allow us express the fact that the CAPEC-34 attack may be initiated with different likelihoods against feature A or feature B.

4.3   Refinement by Element Merging

The opposite of refinement of splitting is refinement by merging. If threat scenarios or unwanted incidents in the risk model describe similar phenomena, then we should consider merging them. For the risk model which is generated from the CAPEC instances, it may be particularly relevant to merge the unwanted incidents describing consequences of CAPEC attacks, since many attacks have the same kinds of consequences. For instance, in Fig. 5, there are two unwanted incidents called *Gain privileges/assume identify due to CAPEC-34 attack* and *Gain privileges/assume identify due to CAPEC-62 attack*. These unwanted incidents represent the same kind of consequence and they differ only in the manner of initiation, and we may therefore consider merging these into one unwanted incident.

4.4   Refinement by Element Addition

The final kind of refinement that we will consider is refinement by element addition. This kind of refinement may be particularly relevant for defining new risks that are specific to the target of evaluation. All unwanted incidents in a risk model derived from CAPEC instances correspond to technical impacts which are described in a quite general manner. Defining new unwanted incidents which are more specific to the target of evaluation and that can be caused by the technical impacts may therefore be relevant. In addition to this, if many CAPEC instances are transformed into a risk model, then we can potentially end up with a great number of possible risks (recall that a risk corresponds to an unwanted incident that harms an asset). Therefore focusing the risk assessment on a few risks which are specific to the target of evaluation is a good way of making the risk model more manageable.

An example of this is given in Fig. 6 where the risk model of Fig. 5 has been refined by adding three new unwanted incidents to the risk model (as shown on the far right of the diagram), and connecting these to the old unwanted incidents and the assets.

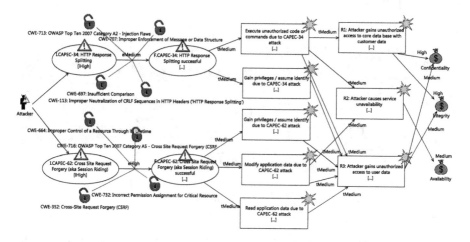

Fig. 6. Example of refinement by element addition

5   Step III: From Specific Risk Models to Test Procedures

The purpose of this step is to identify and prioritize test procedures that can be used as starting point for a security test design activity. This step has two tasks

- Determine whether testing is necessary
- If testing is necessary, use technique **T2** to generate and prioritize test procedures based on the risk models.

The technique **T2** is defined elsewhere [14], however we will discuss its use here for purpose of self-containment and for arguing that the risk model obtained from CAPEC translation is a suitable starting point for test procedure identification.

To determine whether testing is necessary, it is useful to represent the risks of a CORAS risk model in a *risk matrix*. Such a risk matrix can be automatically generated from the risk model given that we have defined all likelihood values precisely and that we have a risk model that is complete in the sense that all initial threat scenarios and all edges/transitions have been given likelihood values. An example of a risk matrix with the three risks R1 - R3 (shown on the right side of Fig. 6) is given in Fig. 7.

Here the vertical axis shows the consequence scale and the horizontal axis shows the likelihood scale. The likelihoods of the risks are given as intervals, i.e. the left hand side of the boxes indicates the minimum likelihood of the intervals, and the right hand side indicates the maximum likelihoods. This should be understood as an expression of the belief that the actual likelihood of the risks lies somewhere within these intervals without knowing precisely where. In the risk matrix of Fig. 7, the diagonal line separates the area into two risk values: *Acceptable* and *Unacceptable*. We see that risk $R1$ is *Unacceptable*, risk $R3$ is *Acceptable*, and $R2$ can be either *Acceptable* or *Unacceptable* depending on what its actual likelihood is.

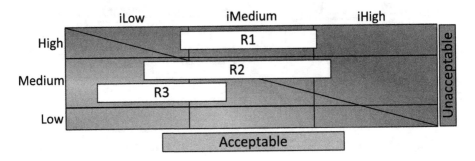

Fig. 7. Risk matrix

How can we use the risk matrix to determine whether testing is necessary? In our view, in the context of risk-based testing, testing can be used a means of gaining knowledge which allows us to estimate the likelihoods of risks and their causes more accurately. In our view, testing is most useful/beneficial if the knowledge acquired through testing could lead to a change in decision making based on risks.

In the current example, the knowledge obtained from testing may be expressed as a narrowing of the likelihood intervals of the risks. If we assume that the decision on how to treat the identified risks is entirely based on their risk value, then testing is necessary it could help us determine a risks risk value more accurately. This means that the decision of whether to test or not is based on the uncertainty of the estimates of the risk model as opposed to the severity of risks. For instance, even though risk $R1$ is considered *Unacceptable* there is no need to obtain new information through testing to reduce the size of the likelihood interval because this will not change the risk value of the risk. However, risk $R2$ is a different matter, it spans both the acceptable and the unacceptable area, thus the problem is not necessarily that the risk is unacceptable, but that we do not know whether it is acceptable or not. For risk $R2$, it makes sense to perform testing to gain new knowledge that allows us to determine whether $R2$ should be treated or not.

If we decide that testing is necessary, the next task is to use technique **T2** for test prioritization and selection to generate a prioritized set of test procedures from the risk model. A risk model can be seen as a set of statements about the world. Testing a risk model corresponds to checking the degree to which these statements are correct. Given a risk model, the first question we must ask is which of its kinds of statements are the most natural starting point for test identification? As discussed further in [14], we believe that the statements derived from edges of a risk model are the most natural starting point. An edges going from a node A to a node B with conditional likelihood l means that "A leads to B with conditional likelihood l", thus a test procedure corresponding to this edge is a statement of the form "Check that A leads to B with conditional likelihood l".

Potentially, every edge of risk model gives rise to a test procedure. However, in practice we do not have time to test every one of these test procedures. Thus we have to prioritize and then select the test procedures that are most important. To achieve this, we must for each edge of a risk model ask whether its corresponding test procedure is within the scope of the risk assessment, and if yes, estimate the resources/effort it would require to implement and execute the test procedure. Subsequently, given an estimate of maximum total effort available for testing, we can use the technique described in [14] to obtain a prioritized list of test procedures that should be implemented and tested. In the following, we illustrate this in an example.

Assume we want to identify test procedures on the basis of the risk model shown in Fig. 6. Our first task is to check whether the test procedure corresponding to each edge of the risk model is within the scope of the assessment, and if yes, estimate the time it will take to test it. Assuming that we are only interested in performing software security testing, then the two edges going from the threat scenarios describing attack initiation to successful attacks are the most natural starting point for testing. Assume that we estimate the time it takes to implement and execute these tests procedures to 1 day each, and that we only have 1 day in total available for doing the testing. We are thus forced to choose which one of the test procedures to test. In order to decide this, we use our technique for test procedure prioritization described in [14], and automatically obtain the test procedures and their priority values as shown in Table 4. Since the first test procedure has a higher priority than the second, we choose the first as the test procedure to test. We believe that the test procedures of Table 4 are a suitable starting point for security test design. In general, we believe that the risk models generated from CAPEC instances (other than the ones shown in the example) are on a suitable level of abstraction for test procedure identification. This is particularly the case for the test procedures derived from edges describing the likelihood of successful CAPEC attacks and the vulnerabilities that may be exploited for this purpose.

6   Related Work

The Common Weakness Risk Analysis Framework (CWRAF) [11] is similar to our work. CWRAF builds on the Common Weakness Scoring System (CWSS)

Table 4. Prioritized list of test procedures

Priority	Test procedure	Severity
1	Check that Cross Site Request Forgery (aka Session Riding) leads to Cross Site Request Forgery (aka Session Riding) successful with conditional likelihood [0.001, 0.1], due to vulnerabilities OWASP Top Ten 2007 Category A5 - Cross Site Request Forgery (CSRF), Incorrect Permission Assignment for Critical Resource, Cross-Site Request Forgery (CSRF) and Improper Control of a Resource Through its Lifetime.	2.138E-4
2	Check that HTTP Response Splitting leads to HTTP Response Splitting successful with conditional likelihood [$1.0E - 4, 0.001$], due to vulnerabilities Insufficient Comparison, Improper Neutralization of CRLF Sequences in HTTP Headers ('HTTP Response Splitting'), Improper Enforcement of Message or Data Structure and OWASP Top Ten 2007 Category A2 - Injection Flaws	3.152E-8

and provide a way of customizing the CWSS scores to specific business domains, technologies or environments. This framework is similar to ours in that it is related to CAPEC (both CAPEC and CWRAF reference the same weaknesses) and that it can be used for the purpose of prioritization. However, the main difference between our approach and CWRAF is that we take likelihood values into account, whereas CWRAF on addresses consequences/impacts only. Thus CWRAF can be considered a more lightweight approach than ours. Another difference is that CWRAF is used to prioritize *weaknesses* and not *attack patterns* as we do.

There are approaches that are similar to ours in that they address the automatic generation of risk models. However, none of the approaches we are aware of take CAPEC as input. For instance, Sheyner et al. [15] proposes an approach for automated generation and analysis of attack graphs. However, the approach assumes a formally defined safety property as input which in our opinion may limit the applicability of the approach. Similarly, Phillips and Swiler [13] also propose an approach for automatically generating attack graphs. The approach assumes as input a network configuration file describing a network topology, a set of attacker profiles, and a set of attack templates. Based on these inputs, an attack graph can be generated. The approach differs from ours in that is addresses *network attacks*, and that it is based on a description of a network topology.

There are many approaches that combine risk assessment and testing. See [3,5] for a survey of the literature in the area. Almost all the approaches to risk-based testing use risk assessment in one of two ways. Either (I) the risk assessment is used to prioritize those parts/features of the system under test that are most risky, or (II) risk assessment is used to identify tests (often as part of a failure/threat identification process). Our approach fits best into category (II). Other approaches that fall into this category are Murthy et al. [12], Zech et al. [16,17], Casado et al. [4], Kumar et al. [7], and Gleirscher [6]. However, none of these approaches use the risk assessment results for test prioritization and none of them consider the automated generation of risk models based on CAPEC.

7   Conclusion and Future Work

We have presented a method for risk-based testing that takes a set of CAPEC attack patterns as input and produces a risk model and a prioritized list of test procedures that can be used as a starting point for security testing. We have describe a technique for automating the construction of the risk model and shown how or method can be used in combination with a technique for test identification and prioritization.

We believe our method supports criteria **C1** - **C3** as described in Sect. 2. In particular, criterion **C1** is supported by our technique **T1** for risk model generation which reduces the time of constructing the risk model compared to a traditional manual process. Criterion **C2** is supported since the generated risk model is suitable for test procedure identification as argued in Sect. 5. Criteria **C3** is supported since our method provides a sound basis for test-procedure prioritization based on risk model information. This enables the testing to be focused on the attacks and/or vulnerabilities that are most relevant for obtaining an accurate and correct risk model.

As part of future work, we plan to further develop our proof-of-concept tools supporting our techniques, and unify these into a single tool which will support both risk model analysis (such as consistency checking, likelihood calculation, and risk visualization), risk model generation from CAPEC, and test identification and prioritization.

Acknowledgments. This work has been conducted as a part of EU project RASEN (316853) funded by the European Commission within the 7th Framework Program.

References

1. ISO 31000:2009(E): Risk management - Principles and guidelines (2009)
2. ISO/IEEE 29119: Software and system engineering - software testing-Part 1–4 (2012)
3. Alam, M.M., Khan, A.I.: Risk-based testing techniques: a perspective study. Int. J. Comput. Appl. **65**(1), 42–49 (2013)
4. Casado, R., Tuya, J., Younas, M.: Testing long-lived web services transactions using a risk-based approach. In: Proceedings of 10th International Conference on Quality Software (QSIC), pp. 337–340. IEEE Computer Society (2010)
5. Erdogan, G., Li, Y., Runde, R.K., Seehusen, F., Stølen, K.: Approaches for the combined use of risk analysis and testing: a systematic literature review. STTT **16**(5), 627–642 (2014)
6. Gleirscher, M.: Hazard-based selection of test cases. In: Proceedings of the 6th International Workshop on Automation of Software Test, pp. 64–70. ACM (2011)

7. Kumar, N., Sosale, D., Konuganti, S.N., Rathi, A.: Enabling the adoption of aspects - testing aspects: a risk model, fault model and patterns. In: Proceedings of the 8th ACM International Conference on Aspect-oriented Software Development, AOSD 2009, pp. 197–206. ACM (2009)
8. Lund, M.S., Solhaug, B., Stølen, K.: Model Driven Risk Analysis - The CORAS Approach. Springer, Heidelberg (2011)
9. MITRE.: Common Attack Pattern Enumeration and Classification (CAPEC) (2015). https://capec.mitre.org (Accessed 30 March 2015)
10. MITRE.: Common Weakness Enumeration (CWE) (2015). https://cwe.mitre.org (Accessed 14 April 2015)
11. MITRE.: Common Weakness Risk Analysis Framework (CWRAF) (2015). https://cwe.mitre.org/cwraf/ (Accessed 30 March 2015)
12. Murthy, K.K., Thakkar, K.R., Laxminarayan, S.: Leveraging risk based testing in enterprise systems security validation. In: Proceedings of the First International Conference on Emerging Network Intelligence, pp. 111–116. IEEE Computer Society (2009)
13. Phillips, C., Swiler, L.P.: A graph-based system for network-vulnerability analysis. In: Proceedings of the 1998 Workshop on New Security Paradigms, NSPW 1998, pp. 71–79. ACM, New York (1998)
14. Seehusen, F.: A technique for risk-based test procedure identification, prioritization and selection. In: Margaria, T., Steffen, B. (eds.) ISoLA 2014, Part II. LNCS, vol. 8803, pp. 277–291. Springer, Heidelberg (2014)
15. Sheyner, O., Haines, J., Jha, S., Lippmann, R., Wing, J.M.: Automated generation and analysis of attack graphs. In: Proceedings of the 2002 IEEE Symposium on Security and Privacy, SP 2002, pp. 273–284. IEEE Computer Society, Washington (2002)
16. Zech, P., Felderer, M., Breu, R.: Towards a model based security testing approach of cloud computing environments. In: 2012 IEEE Sixth International Conference on Software Security and Reliability Companion (SERE-C), pp. 47–56. IEEE (2012)
17. Zech, P., Felderer, M., Breu, R.: Towards risk - driven security testing of service centric systems. In: QSIC, pp. 140–143. IEEE (2012)

Risk-Driven Vulnerability Testing: Results from eHealth Experiments Using Patterns and Model-Based Approach

Alexandre Vernotte[1]($\boxtimes$), Cornel Botea[2], Bruno Legeard[1,3], Arthur Molnar[2,4], and Fabien Peureux[1,3]

[1] Institut FEMTO-ST, UMR CNRS 6174, Route de Gray, 25030 Besançon, France
{avernott,blegeard,fpeureux}@femto-st.fr
[2] Info World, Intrarea Glucozei nr. 37-39, Sector 2, 023828 Bucuresti, Romania
{cornel.botea,arthur.molnar}@infoworld.ro
[3] Smartesting Solutions & Services, 18, rue Alain Savary, 25000 Besançon, France
{legeard,peureux}@smartesting.com
[4] Babes-Bolyai University, Mihail Kogalniceanu nr. 1, Cluj-Napoca, Romania
arthur@cs.ubbcluj.ro

Abstract. This paper introduces and reports on an original tooled risk-driven security testing process called Pattern-driven and Model-based Vulnerability Testing. This fully automated testing process, drawing on risk-driven strategies and Model-Based Testing (MBT) techniques, aims to improve the capability of detection of various Web application vulnerabilities, in particular SQL injections, Cross-Site Scripting, and Cross-Site Request Forgery. It is based on a mixed modeling of the system under test: an MBT model captures the behavioral aspects of the Web application, while formalized vulnerability test patterns, selected from risk assessment results, drive the overall test generation process. An empirical evaluation, conducted on a complex and freely-accessible eHealth system developed by Info World, shows that this novel process is appropriate for automatically generating and executing risk-driven vulnerability test cases and is promising to be deployed for large-scale Web applications.

Keywords: Risk-driven testing · Vulnerability testing · Security test pattern · eHealth web application · Empirical evaluation

1 Introduction

The ubiquity of computer systems in the form of notebooks, tablet PCs and smartphones, backed by continued investment in high-speed data networks have led to a digital world that is dominated by complex, large-scale networked systems exchanging large amounts of information. Furthermore, a new generation of digitally-knowledgeable users have raised expectations from the computer systems they use. For software vendors, meeting these expectations brings increased revenue but also increased risk; a combination of programming errors

© Springer International Publishing Switzerland 2015
F. Seehusen et al. (Eds.): RISK 2015, LNCS 9488, pp. 93–109, 2015.
DOI: 10.1007/978-3-319-26416-5_7

and malicious users can lead to corruption or theft of user data, followed by loss of reputation, business and money [1].

These aspects are even more poignant in the case of companies active in domains such as finance or healthcare, where the consequences of data breaches are magnified by the sensitive nature of the data [2]. This is the case for Info World[1], the largest company specialized in eHealth software development in Romania. Info World provides a complete product stack that includes solutions for management of clinical and financial processes for over 100 customers in Romania and abroad including hospitals, private clinics, pharmacies and clinical laboratories. Info World is also the developer of the Medipedia Web platform[2], that allows users to freely create and manage their electronic healthcare record. As such, the company must find a continuous balance between a fast release cycle required by increasing user expectations on one hand and the usability and security of its provided solutions on the other.

Like all eHealth players on the EU market, Info World observes current regulations pertaining to the protection of personal data, currently represented by the 95/46/EC Directive that were adopted in Romania via Law 677/2001. However, the mid 2010's are a time of crossroads with regards to data privacy, as new regulations regarding the protection of personal data are expected to come into effect in the form of the General Data Protection Regulation (GDPR) sometime after 2015 [3]. The GDPR is expected to provide an updated legal framework accounting for the effect of disruptive technologies such as rich Internet applications and cloud services. Coming into effect in a time frame where data breaches are becoming common as shown in [1], its adoption will require companies such as Info World to recalibrate their efforts to be compliant with upcoming regulations that have an effect on the technical implementation of security features.

The latest draft of the GDPR article 31 specifies that all data breaches, regardless of caused prejudice must be reported to the supervisory authority within 24 h, which changes the impact of data breaches independently of prejudice. This is compounded by increased administrative sanctions outlined in article 79, which can now reach 2 % of annual worldwide turnover. The draft also introduces new classifications relevant for eHealth data are included such as *genetic data*, *biometric data* and *data concerning health* that will impact data controllers handling healthcare information. Furthermore, the draft also introduces the term "explicit consent", with data controllers such as Info World bearing the burden of proof for the data subject's consent.

The combination between complex networked systems and a changing legal landscape requires companies to develop and adopt actionable means for security risk assessment. Within the European FP7 RASEN project[3], we propose an original testing process guided by risk assessment (by means of risk coverage) to address this issue and to automate vulnerability testing for large-scale Web applications. This process, called Pattern-driven and Model-based Vulnerability

---

[1] http://www.infoworld.ro/en_index.html.

[2] http://www.medipedia.ro/.

[3] http://www.rasenproject.eu/.

Testing (PMVT for short), extends Model-Based Testing techniques by driving the testing process using security test patterns selected from risk assessment.

Hence, the purpose and the contribution of the present paper are to introduce the PMVT testing process and to examine its benefits and weaknesses during experimental evaluation on the eHealth Medipedia system developed by Info World. The paper is organized as follows. We start by providing background and we introduce the risk-driven PMVT process in Sect. 2. Section 3 details the Medipedia Web portal, and the related input testing artefacts developed to apply the PMVT process on Medipedia are provided. Section 4 gives the empirical results and the lessons learned from these experiments. Finally, we conclude and suggest ideas for improvement and future work in Sect. 5.

2   Background and Overview of the PMVT Process

The proposed PMVT process is tightly coupled with model-based testing (MBT), vulnerability testing, and obviously risk-driven testing. This section recalls the basics of these techniques, and briefly introduces the PMVT process.

2.1   Model-Based Testing

Model-Based Testing (MBT) [4] is a software testing approach in which both test cases and expected results are automatically derived from an abstract model of the system under test (SUT). More precisely, MBT techniques derive abstract test cases (including stimuli and expected outputs) from an MBT model, which formalizes the behavioral aspects of the SUT in the context of its environment and at a given level of abstraction. The test cases generated from such models allow the validation of the functional aspects of the SUT by comparing back-to-back the results observed on the SUT with those specified by the MBT model. MBT is usually performed to automate and rationalize functional black-box testing. It is a widely-used approach that has gained much interest in recent years, from academic as well as industrial domains, especially by increasing and mastering test coverage, including support for certification, and by providing the degree of automation needed for accelerating the test process [5].

2.2   Vulnerability Testing

Based on the current state of the art on security and on all the security reports such as in the OWASP Top Ten weaknesses 2013 [6] and 2013 CWE/SANS 25 [7], Web applications are the most popular targets when speaking of cyber-attacks. Moreover, the mosaic of technologies in current Web applications increases the risk of security breaches, whereas application-level vulnerabilities are growing.

Application-level vulnerability testing is traditionally performed by developers, but they often lack the in-depth knowledge in recent vulnerabilities and related exploits. These kind of tests can also be achieved by companies specialized in areas of security testing such as penetration testing. But they mainly use manual approaches, making the dissemination of their techniques very difficult, and the impact of this knowledge very low. Finally, Web application vulnerability scanners can be used to automate the detection of vulnerabilities, but since they often generate many false positive and false negative results, human investigation is also required [8].

2.3 Risk-Driven Testing

Risk and requirements-driven testing was originally introduces by James Bach in [9], where he underlined the creative aspects of software testing to manage stated and unstated requirements depending on risks associated with the SUT. This means going beyond having just one test for each stated requirement and implies abilities from the Quality Assurance team to recognize potential risks for the SUT. Risk may be defined as an unwanted incident, which may occur at a given likelihood and impact an asset with a given consequence. Risk-driven test process management focuses on risk assessment and test prioritization based on requirements. This approach influences the entire MBT testing process by driving the development of test generation artefacts: (1) MBT models have to precisely capture risk aspects besides functional features, and (2) the test selection strategies applied on MBT models have to be specified to cover risk and its related priorities. The next subsection introduces the PMVT process, which implements these features to enable risk-driven MBT approach.

2.4 Overview of the PMVT Test Generation Method

The PMVT testing process, depicted in Fig. 1, aims to derive test cases from risk assessment results. These results, which identify threat scenarios, can be informal or specified using a more formal approach such as the CORAS [10]

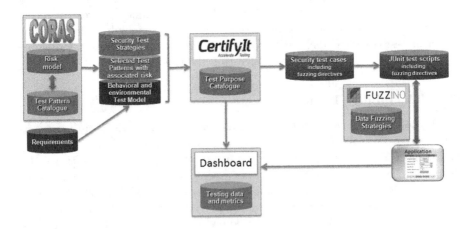

Fig. 1. Pattern-driven and model-based vulnerability testing process

method with risk models. Within the PMVT process, such results are used to select related testing criteria in the form of security test patterns, which define the testing strategy to be applied on the MBT model to derive vulnerability test cases. MBT models are written using a Domain Specific Modeling Language (DSML), called DASTML, that makes the MBT model focusing on SUT behaviors required to apply the risk-driven strategies. Abstract test cases are generated using MBT with Smartesting *CertifyIt* [11] (to derive test sequences) and fuzzing with Fraunhofer FOKUS's library *Fuzzino* [12] (to instantiate attack vectors). Finally, test scripts are generated and executed against the SUT.

Due to space restrictions it is not possible to give a complete and thorough description of this risk-driven process; instead, we refer the interested reader to the detailed overview of the PMVT process available in [13]. However, in order to allow a better understanding of the rest of the paper, the next paragraphs emphasise the testing artefacts involved in PMVT test case generation, test script derivation and test execution.

Test Pattern. Within PMVT process, risk analysis provides a selection and a prioritization of threat scenarios with respect to risk estimation. Such scenarios, typically addressing the OWASP Top Ten vulnerabilities, are linked to one or several security test patterns [14], which express the testing procedure to identify the corresponding threat in a Web application.

Test Purpose. The *CertifyIt* test generation tool provides a catalogue of generic test purposes that formalize test patterns. Basically, a test purpose is a high-level partial algorithm that defines a sequence of significant steps that has to be performed by the test case. Each step takes the form of a set of operations or behaviors to be covered, or specific states to be reached on the MBT model in order to assess the robustness of the SUT regarding the related vulnerability.

MBT Model. The MBT model is provided using a DASTML specification describing the global structure of a Web application: the available pages, the available actions on each page, the user inputs of each action potentially used to inject attack vectors, etc. It embeds all the structural and behavioral entities needed to derive a UML MBT model (native input model of *CertifyIt*) and to generate the intended tests by applying test purposes.

Abstract Test Case. Applying each test purpose on the MBT model produces one or more abstract test cases verifying the test purpose specification and the MBT model constraints. Such an abstract test case takes the form of a sequence of steps, where a step corresponds to an operation call representing either an action or an observation of the SUT.

Executable Test Script. Each abstract test case is exported into the execution environment as a JUnit test case skeleton to create a JUnit test suite.

To bridge the gap between abstract and executable data, a file, containing the prototype of each operation of the SUT, allow the linking between abstract and concrete structures. The test automation engineer is in charge of implementing each operation and data of this interface. Moreover, the JUnit test suite embeds the security test strategies (from security test patterns) that are used by the fuzz test data generation Fuzzino to automatically generate relevant attack vectors to operation arguments. Hence, each abstract test case finally produces several executable JUnit test cases: one for each combination of fuzzed attack vectors.

Test Results. JUnit test cases are finally executed by a JUnit environment supporting its computation on the SUT to assign an execution verdict. Test results are then gathered and displayed in a dashboard that can compute various security testing metrics such as the number of executed test cases, passed or failed, the percentage of the attack surface elements (coverage) that are addressed by the test cases, the characteristics of each used attack vector, the coverage of the paths to execute the attack, etc.

3   Medipedia Case-Study and Related Testing Inputs

In this section we firstly detail the Medipedia Web portal by introducing its main features and the identified security and legal risks. Based on the company's expectations, we next introduce the test generation inputs, i.e. test patterns and DASTML model, used to achieve these objectives with the PMVT process.

3.1   The Medipedia Web Application

The Medipedia Web portal is a complex eHealth system that is accessible by creating a free user profile. The system acts as a Web portal that provides articles and news that are relevant for the prevention, treatment and control of diseases commonly occurring in the Romanian population. Users can access the portal via one of the three roles: public user, registered user or medical personnel. Each role has clearly defined rights and limitations. At the time of writing, the Medipedia community includes over 40.000 registered users as well as over 150.000 weekly visitors, a linear increase of around 20 % from 2014.

Everyone can access the public section that includes the articles section together with medicine brochures, suppliers and a medical forum where they can interact with other users or the registered physicians. In addition, registered users can access their electronic health record that acts as the hub of their electronic healthcare data. As it includes sensitive personal data, access to the health records are provided based on a signed agreement and data is secured via the user's account. Users can provide other users, such as family members or physicians registered within the platform access to some or all of their stored data, on the basis of a signed agreement. Moreover, granting a registered physician temporary access rights is also possible for the purposes of gaining a second opinion.

In this way, physicians can access the patient's medical history in a centralized manner during the patient encounter, with no time or location constraints.

Medical data can be added to a user's record in two ways. First of all, organizations that are interconnected with Medipedia can add the results of medical or laboratory examinations to the user's account automatically and securely, while observing the user's right to privacy. At the time of writing, the Medipedia platform is integrated with Medcenter, a nationwide network of over 40 clinics that provides consultations and laboratory analyses. Medical results obtained outside of the Medcenter network can be added by registered users manually.

Technical and Legal Aspects. The Medipedia portal is part of Info World's portfolio for the management of care and financial processes in clinical units. Together with its systems for management of hospital, laboratory, pharmacy and imagistics processes, Info World solutions cover the entire spectrum of requirements for patient management and care. From a technical standpoint, all Info World products are Health Level 7 (HL7) v3 compliant [15] in order to ensure interoperability between the company's products as well as facilitate integration with components provided by other vendors. In order to facilitate interoperability, reduce software redundancy the HL7 group have defined components that facilitate the management of patients, patient encounters and medical records [16].

The Medipedia platform employs several such components that were developed in-house, but according to HL7 interoperability specifications. A detailed description of these services in a relevant context for Medipedia is available at [17]. The Entity Identification Services (EIS), which manages the involved entities such as external organizations, clinical locations, practitioners and registered users. All medical documents are attached to the account of a user from the EIS service. The management of medical records is handled by the Resource Location and Reporting Service, that implements Integrating the Healthcare Enterprise (IHE)'s XDS Cross Enterprise Document Exchange profile and understands HL7 v3, CDA v2 and DICOM messages [18]. Medical documents uploaded by the user or transferred to their profile by the system are stored within this service. At the base of these services we find the Enterprise Vocabulary Service, which provides common and machine translatable clinical vocabulary services and is employed within all medical documents.

These services can be accessed after authentication and authorization by the Security Service, which uses a role-based access control model. The architecture of the security services itself is compliant with the AuditTrail and Node Authentication, Cross Enterprise User Authentication and Document Digital Signature profiles of the IHE as detailed within [18]. This ensures the confidentiality, integrity and availability of the system, together with recording detailed audit logs that allow post-mortem analysis, with important significance in tracing healthcare decisions. The services environment for Medipedia, including the security components is illustrated in Fig. 2. Physically, the platform is currently deployed in a secured data-centre that is off-site from company locations.

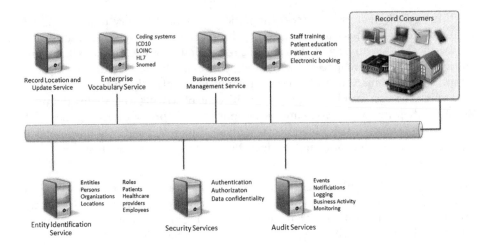

Fig. 2. Medipedia services architecture

Motivation for Risk-Driven Testing. The intersection between eHealth as a business area having particular constraints with regards to privacy and the safekeeping of user data and the rich functionalities required by users, it leads to a level of risk that requires the adoption of latest methodologies and tools for prevention and mitigation. Info World's motivation regarding the adoption of risk-driven testing are two-fold: the large attack surface of the Medipedia Web site, and the reuse of core components across company products.

As a highly visible, feature-rich system Medipedia provides a large attack surface. Any loss of data confidentiality or integrity can bear multiple financial and legal consequences imposed by the National Authority for Data Protection, partner medical clinics or compromised end-users. In addition, since medical decision are taken every day on the basis of the data stored in the system its corruption can have direct and undesirable medical consequence for its users.

Reuse of the core components described in [17] across Info World's solutions reduces development time, testing effort and allows shipping features across products faster. However, software component reuse can increase security risks, as any vulnerability in one of these components is likely to be exploitable across most of the company's product stack.

As such, we believe that an automated and composable tool-backed methodology for security risk assessment and testing represents the best approach for ensuring the security and integrity of user data. To evaluate the PMVT process, three major attacks have been identified from risk assessment and have been targeted for PMVT test generation purpose:

– SQL injection (SQLI) is the most popular code injection technique, used to attack data-driven applications. To achieve this kind of attack, malicious SQL statements are inserted into an entry field of a Web page in order to be executed on the database, for example to dump the database contents.

- Cross-site scripting (XSS) is also an injection of malicious executable code into an entry field of a Web page, that stores and executes it in any Web browser that later loads the related page. Therefore, it is possible to inject a piece of code and see this code executed, potentially causing severe damage to visitors and allowing many exploits (hijacking, credential theft, etc.).
- Cross-site request forgery (CSRF) consists of an attacker bringing a user to make HTTP requests, against his will, to a Web site that trusts the user. This can be done for instance using fishing techniques, or by injecting a malicious URL in an image-tag's source attribute of an HTML formatted e-mail that might be automatically followed by the e-mail client software. Thus, the attacker can perform requests with the user's credentials and privileges, because browsers automatically include credentials in every request made to a Web site to simulate statelessness.

In the present paper, the deployment of PMVT on the Medipedia case-study will be mainly illustrated using CSRF attacks. However, the obtained results and lessons learned from these experiments cover our experience regarding the three selected attack types. The next subsections respectively introduce the related test patterns and the DASTML model of the Medipedia Web site.

3.2   Test Patterns Selected from Risk Assessment

The PMVT process exploits test pattern description, selected from risk assessment, by transforming them into formal representation, called test purposes. A Test Patterns is a normalized textual document describing the testing objectives and procedures to detect a particular flaw in a Web application. Hence, there are as many test patterns as there are types of application-level flaws. For example, an excerpt of the test pattern corresponding to the description of the CSRF attack is given in Fig. 3.

The PMVT process takes such textual test pattern as starting point by mapping them into formal directives, called test purposes, in order to automate testing strategy implementation and execution. Such test purposes are generic,

Name	Cross-Site Request Forgery (CSRF)
CWE-ID(s)	CWE-352
Description	The Web application does not, or cannot, sufficiently verify whether a well-formed, valid, consistent request was intentionally provided by the user who submitted the request.
Discussion	When a Web server is designed to receive a request from a client without any mechanism for verifying that it was intentionally sent, then it might be possible for an attacker to trick a client into making an unintentional request to the Web server, which will be treated as an authentic request. This can be done via a URL, image load, XMLHttpRequest, etc. and can result in exposure of data or unintended code execution.
Test Coverage	Interfaces that provide functions requiring authentication
...	...
References	OWASP Top 10 (2013): A8-Cross-Site Request Forgery, CWE-352: Cross-Site Request Forgery (CSRF).

Fig. 3. Excerpt of the test pattern for CSRF attack

meaning they may be applied as it is on any PMVT project. As detailed in the previous section, we propose to apply three test purposes to the Medipedia case-study, each of them targeting a specific vulnerability type: SQLI, XSS and CSRF. It should be noted that two different test purposes enable two test XSS injections: single-step XSS (the malicious injected code is rendered back on the next page) and multi-step XSS (several navigation steps are required to get to the output page). Hence, four test purposes have been executed to cover the three selected types of attacks.

The test purpose language allows the formalization of typical vulnerability test patterns for Web applications. This is a textual language, based on regular expressions, defining vulnerability test intention in terms of states to be reached and operations to be called. Basically, the language relies on combining keywords to produce expressions that are both powerful and easy to read. Both SQL and XSS injections, whose procedures are implemented with this test purpose language, are tackled using the same logic [19]. It consists of reaching the page containing the user input to be tested, injecting malicious code, then observing the result (for multi-step XSS an additional output page has to be defined to precise which operation(s) to call in order to reach that page). To address CSRF, the approach is different and a little bit more complex, as shown in Fig. 4.

```
for_each literal $action from #CSRF_ACTIONS,
use any_operation any_number_of_times to_reach
 "not(self.webAppStructure.ongoingAction.oclIsUndefined())
and   self.webAppStructure.ongoingAction.id=ACTION_IDS::$action"
          on_instance sut
then use threat.gatherCSRFInfo() then use was.finalizeAction()
then use sut.reset()
then use any_operation any_number_of_times to_reach
 "not(self.webAppStructure.ongoingAction.oclIsUndefined())
and   self.webAppStructure.ongoingAction.id=ACTION_IDS::LOGIN"
          on_instance sut then use was.finalizeAction()
then use threat.performCSRFAttack()
then use threat.checkCSRF()
```

Fig. 4. Test purpose for CSRF attack

The algorithm's logic is as follows. On line 1, a *foreach* statement is used to apply the following steps to all actions with an identified risk to CSRF (relying on the MBT model). On line 2, the test purpose indicates to reach a specific state by calling any operations any number of times. The specific state is defined as an OCL constraint, expressing that the current page displayed to the user should be the page containing the action under test. The *gatherCSRFInfo()* method is called on line 3, which gathers information about the resulting page, essentially the page itself, for later use during verdict assignment. This operation has no effect on the model. On line 5, the *reset()* method is called, which basically restores the initial state of the SUT. On line 6, the model is put in a state corresponding to a successful login. The *performCSRFAttack()* is called on line 6, it has not effect on the model but calls for a sub-algorithm in charge of deploying the attack. On line 7, the *checkCSRF()* method is called, no effect on the model again and consists of comparing the page resulting from the attack with the page resulting from the normal execution of the action (stored earlier by the *gatherCSRFInfo()* method). Such test purposes are used in conjunction with an MBT model to automatically generate vulnerability test cases.

3.3   MBT Model for Medipedia Case-Study

Information about the SUT depicted in the MBT model is structural and behavioral: every relevant page is represented and, for each one, a list of actions and navigation links. To address the Medipedia case-study, 25 pages have been modeled, containing in total 20 actions, 47 user inputs, and 28 navigation links.

A fragment of the Medipedia DASTML model, which depicts the page displaying a given forum topic, is shown in Fig. 5. It is composed of two actions. The *POST_ANSWER* action allows a user to post a message related to the topic. This action contains a parameter *PA_CONTENT* valued to *PA_CONTENT_1*. What follow the arrow (=>) are the two output pages rendering the value of the *PA_CONTENT* parameter (this is typically useful for XSS). The absence of arrow (→) in this action means that the user stays on the same page after performing the action. The second action *EDIT_POST* is mostly similar, although it concerns the edition of an existing post rather than the creation of a new one. Despite actions, navigation links are also represented. There is only one link in this model fragment, which takes a user from the forum topic to the forum home page. An MBT model is therefore a set of pages, with links and actions that connect them to each other.

```
"PAT_VIEW_TOPIC" {
     ACTIONS { "POST_ANSWER" ("PA_CONTENT" = "PA_CONTENT_1"
                        => {"AN_VIEW_TOPIC","PAT_VIEW_TOPIC"}),
               "EDIT_POST" ("EP_CONTENT" = "EP_CONTENT_1"
                        => {"AN_VIEW_TOPIC","PAT_VIEW_TOPIC"})
             }
     NAVIGATIONS { "GOTO_PAT_FORUMS" -> "PAT_FORUMS"}
}
```

Fig. 5. DASTML fragment of the view forum topic page of medipedia

Designing the application using the DASTML language took about three hours, without having any prior knowledge of its structure. As a comparison, to evaluate it would have taken at least six hours in order to design the corresponding UML diagrams required by the *CertifyIt* tool. Once the MBT model has been designed and test purposes have been selected, they are provided as inputs to the Smartesting *CertifyIt* test generator to compute abstract test cases. The next section presents and discusses the test generation results computed from the four selected test purposes and the DASTML model of Medipedia.

4   Empirical Results and Lessons Learned

On one hand, this section describes how test cases are generated and executed for the Medipedia case-study and on the other, illustrates the empirical test results and discusses the main lessons learned from these experiments.

4.1   Test Generation Results

MBT model and test purposes are composed using *CertifyIt* to generate abstract test cases. First, the MBT model is translated in a set of constraints. Second, *CertifyIt* unfolds each *for_each* statement of each test purpose. The result is a set of instantiated test purposes. Third, for a given instantiated test purpose, the test generator follows its "road map" (i.e. the set of operations, states and OCL constraints described by the currently-computed instantiated test purpose) by trying to call each operation, reach each state, and satisfy each OCL constraint. Once each step has been fulfilled, an abstract test case is produced.

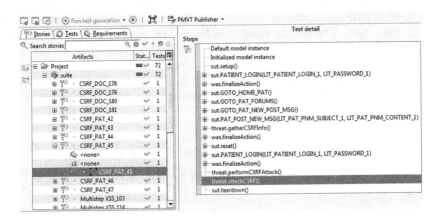

Fig. 6. Example of a CSRF abstract test case from *certifyIt*

A screenshot of the test generation results from Medipedia is shown in Fig. 6. On the left side of the screenshot, a tree list of all the instantiated test purposes is displayed, each representing a test target. On the right side of the screenshot, the ordered set of steps (operation calls), which constitutes the corresponding abstract test case is shown. For example, the test target *CSRF_PAT_45* consists of checking if the action of posting a new forum post is vulnerable to CSRF. This attack trace consists of (i) logging into the application (*PATIENT_LOGIN*), (ii) navigating in the Web application until reaching the injection page (*GOTO_SOMEPAGE*), (iii) providing nominal inputs (*PAT_POST_NEW_MSG*), (iv) gathering information related to CSRF, submitting the form and resetting the application's state (*gatherCSRFInfo(), finalizeAction(), reset()*), (v) logging in as the patient (*PATIENT_LOGIN*), (vi) submitting the form from an external location (*performCSRFAttack()*), and (vii) comparing the two responses from the Web Application to assign a verdict ($checkCSRF()$).

The test generation computation (addressing the four selected test purposes) takes approximately half an hour to provide 85 abstract test cases: 47 for SQLI, 27 for XSS (18 for single-step XSS and 9 for multi-step), and 11 for CSRF.

4.2   Test Execution Results

Abstract test cases cannot be executed on the real Web application, therefore it is required to export the test suite as a set of JUnit test cases. A dedicated exporter has been developed to generate a maven project containing all the needed third party libraries and putting each JUnit test case into a given package. The content of a JUnit test case is pretty similar to an abstract test case in the sense that it describes the set of operation calls that must be manually implemented in a class called *AdapterImplementation*. For example, the abstract test case of Fig. 6 has been exported as a JUnit test case, as shown in Fig. 7.

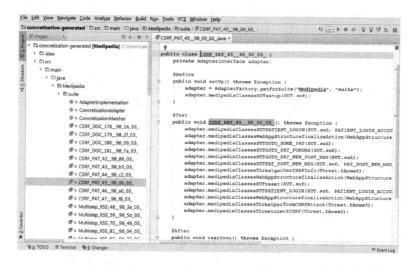

Fig. 7. Example of a CSRF concrete Junit4 test case

The role of the *AdapterImplementation* class is to close the gap between abstract values and operations to concrete values and instrumented operations. Because instrumenting operations is a rather time-consuming yet repetitive activity, an algorithm has been designed to generate basic code for operations, executable as it is for most cases. HTMLUnit is used to simulate user/Web application interactions, by separating behavioral actions into two families: *gotos* actions and *user-supplied inputs* actions. *Gotos* actions consist of a click on some control point that triggers a HTTP request for another page. The exporter generates primitives to find the control point on the current page and to click on it. For *User-supplied inputs* actions, the exporter seeks for each parameter on the current page and sets its corresponding value, again using HTMLUnit primitives. Even if generated primitives may need an extra crafting from the test engineer (usually by adding primitives as a preamble), it has shown to accelerate the concretization activity by dividing its time cost by 2. Nevertheless, it implies that a test engineer is still required to map abstract data with concrete ones: each parameter *id* (form fields, links) and nominal values of the MBT model must be mapped into a concrete value gathered by manually crawling the SUT.

Exporting the abstract test cases of the Medipedia case-study into JUnit test cases, customizing a few generated primitives, and providing concrete values took about six hours. It should be noted that the injection-type attacks (SQLI and XSS) use a list of attack vectors provided by the *Fuzzino* tool: we make use of JUnit parameters to perform the same attack over and over, each time with a different vector. This approach is particularly relevant in the case of XSS because of the almost-infinite ways to conduct an XSS attack, but it is also relevant for SQLI injections since they are closely linked to the kind of DBMS running in the backend, as well as the form of the initial request. Therefore, each SQLI test case is executed 10 times, whereas each XSS test case is executed 105 times. In total, execution took about 45 min for 3316 test cases. Table 1 summarizes the test execution results of the Medipedia case-study.

Table 1. Test execution results of the medipedia case-study

Vulnerability	Abstract test cases	Attack Vectors	Executable test cases	Detected vulnerabilities	False positives	False negatives
SQLI	47	10	470	0	0	0
Single-step XSS	18	105	1890	1	0	12
Multi-step XSS	9	105	945	1	0	12
CSRF	11	1	11	0	2	0

Upon test execution, a multi-step vulnerability was found in the Medipedia forum. Indeed, on the "new forum post as a visitor" page, the name field is vulnerable to XSS because the value of the field is used as output on the "display forum topics" page without proper sanitation. To be effectively detected, this multi-step XSS vulnerability requires a complex verdict assignment process, which is built-it in the PMVT process, and not easy to find using current practices based on scanner inspections. The forum also contains a single-step XSS vulnerability: Again, on the "new forum post as a visitor" page, the content field is vulnerable because its value is rendered back raw on the "display post" page.

Finally, some of the executed tests misreported a vulnerability or missed one. For instance, 24 tests for XSS revealed to be false negatives. This is not alarming since these false negatives came in fact from attack vectors whose purpose is to detect XSS in very specific configurations, which was not the case in Medipedia. In addition, 2 tests targeting CSRF attacks came back positive, but we were not able to reproduce the attack manually. This is further discussed in the next section that deals with the experiments feedback and related discussion.

4.3   Lessons Learned and Discussion

First, MBT techniques are known to be time-consuming, and PMVT is no exception. Of course, the designed DSML clearly eases the modeling activity. The use of an algorithm to infer most parts of the adaptation layer showed its effectiveness as well. However, there is still a significant amount of work to do before getting early results, especially for a consequent Web application like Medipedia. But in the end, merely ten hours were spent on the deployment of PMVT: three hours to model the application, six hours to design the adaptation layer, and one hour to execute the tests and observe the results. We managed to operate within such a short timeframe because we chose to only address vulnerabilities regarded as a major threat according to risk analysis, letting aside other vulnerability kinds considered less threatening. This allowed us to focus solely on SQLI, XSS, and CSRF. Similarly, we relied on risk analysis to only represent the needed information about the most sensible parts of the Medipedia Web site. These choices helped us to considerably reduce the complexity of all PMVT activities. The DASTML language has also shown its effectiveness since it allows engineers to be focused on the information needed for vulnerability testing, avoid spending useless time during modeling, and maintain a scalable MBT model devoid of noisy specified data regarding the test generation process. To reach a better level of automation, we are planning on collecting user traces to infer the model and provide concrete data to the adaptation layer. These traces would consist of a recording when a user uses its browser to explore the SUT and collect relevant information similarly to the Selenium IDE.

Second, the use of the Fuzzino test data generator to instantiate attack vectors on-the-fly during test cases execution makes it possible to execute a large number of test cases without having to manage a lot of similar abstract test cases (that would differ merely in the fuzzed data). Hence, this approach has the advantages of keeping the model clean and externalizing the definition of attack vectors that can be independently updated or parameterized.

Third, executing automated tests using HTMLUnit on Medipedia happened to be problematic, since the developers of Web applications make extensive use of Javascript to handle structure changes in the DOM. HTMLUnit is known to have unsafe behavior when interpreting Javascript, and a few pages could not be accessed with standard GUI navigation. We had to tweak HTMLUnit primitives and hardcode URLs to access these pages. We are investigating alternative way to overcome this issue, such as the use of Selenium, which provides a PhantomJS driver that makes use of real Javascript engines such as WebKit.

Finally, automatic verdict assignment is the "Holly Grail" of software testing. During experiments, 2 tests about CSRF came back positive. Nonetheless, when we tried to reproduce the attack manually, we were unable to reproduce and so to confirm the vulnerability. It means that the technique we use for verdict assignment is not precise enough: we compare the output upon form submission through the GUI with form submission from an external server, using Doupé's control point comparison technique as proposed in [20]. However, while the Medipedia Web site blocks data that it receives from the outside, it redirects users to the same page whether data were sent through the GUI or from an external location (which could be a consequence of a CSRF attack). It tricked our algorithm since the two output pages were alike even though the attack did not work. We are addressing this problem at the time of writing.

5 Conclusion and Further Work

This paper reports on a novel risk-driven testing process called PMVT, that addresses Web application vulnerabilities. This MBT process is based on security test patterns selected from risk assessment, and behavioral models of the SUT described by a dedicated Domain-Specific Modeling Language (DASTML). The generic formalization of the test patterns into high-level expressions called test purposes enables to efficiently automate the testing process by guiding test generation. DASTML modeling makes it possible to describe the necessary information of the Web application under test, and also contributes to ease and accelerate the whole process. We make use of the *CertifyIt* test generator to compose models and test purposes in order to generate a suite of abstract test cases, which are next exported as JUnit test case and fuzzed to be executed on SUT. To improve this concretization step, a developed exporter generates most part of the Adaptation layer, which implements operations from the DASTML model with HTMLUnit primitives. The experiments conducted on the real-life and complex eHealth Medipedia system have demonstrated that the PMVT process provides effective benefits, in particular by finding an undiscovered XSS vulnerability in the forum of the application. This empirical evaluation has also underlined further work, for example, the need to improve the verdict assignment for CSRF detection in order to avoid false positives, and recording user traces in order to even better ease and accelerate the MBT modeling activity.

Acknowledgement. This work is supported by the European FP7 project RASEN, which aims to provide risk-driven security testing techniques for large-scale networked systems.

References

1. Hong, J., Linden, G.: Protecting against data breaches; living with mistakes. Commun. ACM **55**(6), 10–11 (2012)
2. Oladimeji, E.A., Chung, L., Jung, H.T., Kim, J.: Managing security and privacy in ubiquitous ehealth information interchange. In: Ubiquitous Information Management and Communication, pp. 1–10. ACM, New York (2011)
3. EU: GDP Regulation Draft (2012). http://ec.europa.eu/justice/data-protection/document/review2012/com_2012_11_en.pdf. Accessed April 2015
4. Utting, M., Legeard, B.: Practical Model-Based Testing - A tools approach. Morgan Kaufmann, San Francisco (2006)
5. Dias-Neto, A., Travassos, G.: A Picture from the model-based testing area: concepts, techniques, and challenges. In: Advances in Computers, vol. 80, pp. 45–120, July 2010. ISSN: 0065-2458

6. Wichers, D.: Open web application security project (2013). https://www.owasp.org/index.php/Category:OWASP_Top_Ten_Project. Accessed April 2015

7. MITRE: Common weakness enumeration, October 2013. http://cwe.mitre.org/. Accessed April 2015

8. Doupé, A., Cova, M., Vigna, G.: Why Johnny can't pentest: an analysis of black-box web vulnerability scanners. In: Kreibich, C., Jahnke, M. (eds.) DIMVA 2010. LNCS, vol. 6201, pp. 111–131. Springer, Heidelberg (2010)

9. Bach, J.: Risk and requirements-based testing. Computer **32**(6), 113–114 (1999). IEEE Press

10. Lund, M.S., Solhaug, B., Stølen, K.: Model-Driven Risk Analysis: The CORAS Approach. 1st edn. Springer Publishing Company, Incorporated (2010)

11. Bouquet, F., Grandpierre, C., Legeard, B., Peureux, F.: A test generation solution to automate software testing. In: Proceedings of the 3rd International Workshop on Automation of Software Test (AST 2008), Leipzig, Germany, pp. 45–48. ACM Press, May 2008

12. Fraunhofer FOKUS: Fuzzing library Fuzzino on Github (2013). https://github.com/fraunhoferfokus/Fuzzino. Accessed April 2015

13. Botella, J., Legeard, B., Peureux, F., Vernotte, A.: Risk-based vulnerability testing using security test patterns. In: Margaria, T., Steffen, B. (eds.) ISoLA 2014, Part II. LNCS, vol. 8803, pp. 337–352. Springer, Heidelberg (2014)

14. Vouffo Feudjio, A.G.: Initial Security Test Pattern Catalog. Public Deliverable D3.WP4.T1, Diamonds Project, Berlin, Germany, June 2012. http://publica.fraunhofer.de/documents/N-212439.html. Accessed February 2014

15. Andrikopoulos, P.K., Belsis, P.: Towards effective organization of medical data. In: Proceedings of the 17th Panhellenic Conference on Informatics (PCI 2013), Thessaloniki, Greece, pp. 305–310. ACM (2013)

16. Eichelberg, M., Aden, T., Riesmeier, J., Dogac, A., Laleci, G.B.: A survey and analysis of electronic healthcare record standards. ACM Comput. Surv. **37**(4), 277–315 (2005)

17. Werner, F.: RASEN Deliverable D2.1.1 - Use Case Scenarios Definition, October 2013. http://www.rasenproject.eu/downloads/723/. Accessed April 2015

18. IHE International: HIE security and privacy through IHE profiles. White paper, IHE IT Infrastructure, August 2008. http://www.ihe.net/Technical_Framework/upload/IHE_ITI_Whitepaper_Security_and_Privacy_of_HIE_2008-08-22-2.pdf. Accessed March 2015

19. Vernotte, A., Dadeau, F., Lebeau, F., Legeard, B., Peureux, F., Piat, F.: Efficient detection of multi-step cross-site scripting vulnerabilities. In: Prakash, A., Shyamasundar, R. (eds.) ICISS 2014. LNCS, vol. 8880, pp. 358–377. Springer, Heidelberg (2014)

20. Doupé, A., Cavedon, L., Kruegel, C., Vigna, G.: Enemy of the state: a state-aware black-box web vulnerability scanner. In: Proceedings of the 21st USENIX Conference on Security Symposium (Security 2012), Bellevue, WA, USA, pp. 523–537. USENIX Association, August 2012

Improving Security Testing with Usage-Based Fuzz Testing

Martin A. Schneider[1]([⊠]), Steffen Herbold[2], Marc-Florian Wendland[1],
and Jens Grabowski[2]

[1] Fraunhofer FOKUS, Berlin, Germany
{martin.schneider,marc-florian.wendland}@fokus.fraunhofer.de
[2] Institute of Computer Science, University of Göttingen, Göttingen, Germany
{herbold,grabowksi}@cs.uni-goettingen.de

Abstract. Along with the increasing importance of software systems for our daily life, attacks on these systems may have a critical impact. Since the number of attacks and their effects increases the more systems are connected, the secure operation of IT systems becomes a fundamental property. In the future, this importance will increase, due to the rise of systems that are directly connected to our environment, e.g., cyber-physical systems and the Internet of Things. Therefore, it is inevitable to find and fix security-relevant weaknesses as fast as possible. However, established automated security testing techniques such as fuzzing require significant computational effort. In this paper, we propose an approach to combine security testing with usage-based testing in order to increase the efficiency of security testing. The main idea behind our approach is to utilize that little tested parts of a system have a higher probability of containing security-relevant weaknesses than well tested parts. Since the execution of a system by users can also be to some degree being seen as testing, our approach plans to focus the fuzzing efforts such that little used functionality and/or input data are generated. This way, fuzzing is targeted on weakness-prone areas which in turn should improve the efficiency of the security testing.

Keywords: Security testing · Fuzzing · Usage-based testing

1 Introduction

Security testing is about finding potential security-relevant weaknesses in the interface of a System Under Test (SUT). In the last decade, vulnerabilities and their exploitation by hacker groups, industrial competitors, and adversary intelligence services became part of our daily lives. This makes it inevitable to detect and fix security-relevant weaknesses as fast as possible. This need will gain much more importance in the future due to the increasing connectivity of systems with real-world entities, e.g., with the emergence of cyber-physical systems and the Internet of Things. The effort required for the security testing with currently established techniques increases dramatically with the complexity of the systems.

© Springer International Publishing Switzerland 2015
F. Seehusen et al. (Eds.): RISK 2015, LNCS 9488, pp. 110–119, 2015.
DOI: 10.1007/978-3-319-26416-5_8

To cope with this problem and to meet the higher requirements with respect to system quality, in particular security, the existing techniques have to become more efficient than they currently are and new techniques have to be devised. In this paper, we want to discuss a new approach based on the combination of fuzzing and usage-based testing in order to provide an automated way yielding an improved efficiency of security testing.

2 Related Work

Since we are combining several existing techniques, we present the chosen and alternative techniques.

2.1 Risk Analysis Appraches

There are several approaches aiming at identifying and assessing risks for certain failures. Fault-Tree Analysis (FTA) [1] is a top down approach. The analysis starts from an undesired state, subsequently exploring different faults and their interrelationships being expressed using logical gates. FTA enables both, qualitative and quantitative analysis.

In contrast to FTA, Failure Mode and Effects Analysis (FMEA) [2] is usually performed as a bottom up approach. Therefore, it does not start from an undesired state but from a malfunctioning component. Thus, the consequences of a component error are analyzed. If a criticality analysis is performed afterwards, it is called Failure Model Effects and Criticality Analysis (FMECA). As FTA, FMEA/FMECA enables qualitative and quantitative analysis.

Attack trees [3] are an approach with some similarity to FTA but fitted to the analysis of security risks. It takes into account the capabilities of an attacker and starts with the goal of an attack as a root node of the tree. The leafs constitute the attacks in order to achieve the goal connected via logical nodes. In additional to FTA, countermeasures can be included in the nodes.

CORAS [4] is an approach for model-based risk assessment, in particular used for security risk analysis. Whereas the aforementioned approaches are based on trees, during the risk analysis according to the CORAS method, graphs are created. The CORAS method comprises eight steps that lead to different kind of diagrams. The approach starts with the analysis of the assets wort protecting, followed by threat identification and estimation and the identification of treatments. CORAS diagrams provide different kind of nodes for threats, e.g., attackers, threat scenarios, vulnerabilities, unwanted incidents, i.e. the result of a successful attack, and considers likelihoods of, e.g., threat scenarios, and impacts on the assets.

All the presented approaches for risk analysis have in common the need for manual analysis performed by system and domain experts, which may require substantial effort.

2.2 Fuzzing

An established technique for finding security weaknesses is fuzzing [5]. Fuzzing is performed in an automated manner and means to stimulate the interface of a SUT with invalid or unexpected inputs. Therefore, it is a negative testing approach. Fuzzing aims at finding missing or faulty input validation mechanisms. This may lead to security-relevant weaknesses if such data is processed instead of being rejected. For instance, a buffer overflow vulnerability usually results from the lack of a length check of user input data. Thus, arbitrary long data can overwrite existing data in system memory and an attacker may use this for code injection. Due to the huge size of the input space, fuzzing research focuses on approaches of how to sample input data in a way that the likelihood of finding weaknesses is high. The existing approaches discussed cover randomly generated data [6] and model-based approaches where models and grammars describe valid and/or invalid input data [5]. Model-based fuzzers have knowledge about the protocol of the interface they are stimulating and are able to generate so-called semi-valid input data. This is data that is mostly valid but invalid in small parts. This allows checking the input validation mechanisms one after another. In order to detect a buffer overflow vulnerability, input data of invalid length would be generated in order to check if the length of input data is verified. However, even with such model-based techniques, the total number of generated inputs usually cannot be tested exhaustively due to time and resource limitations.

Recently, behavioral models have also been considered for fuzzing [7]. With behavioral fuzzing, invalid message sequences are generated instead of invalid data. For example, this can lead to finding weaknesses in authentication mechanisms, where the exact order of messages is relevant. However, this procedure also leads to a huge number of behavioral variations where executing all of them is usually infeasible due to a lack of time and resources.

As described above, the number of invalid inputs generated by fuzzing techniques is usually too large to execute all as tests. The challenge is to select those test cases that have a high probability of finding a weakness. While there are approaches to cope with this manually, e.g., risk-based security testing [8], the automated selection is still an unresolved research topic.

2.3 Usage-Based Testing

Usage-based testing is an approach for software testing that focuses the usage of a system. Instead of testing all parts of the system equally, the parts that are often used are tested intensively, while seldom or never used parts are ignored [9]. The foundation for usage-based testing are usage profiles, i.e., stochastic descriptions of the user behavior, usually as some form of Markov process (e.g., [10]). The usage profile is inferred from a usage journal which is collected by a monitor observing the SUT during its operation. The journal also contains the data users sent. Sensitive user data, e.g., names and passwords, are filtered from this data. This can be achieved by ignoring the values of certain observed elements, e.g., password fields or the tagging of fields that contain sensitive data, e.g., name fields.

3   Our Approach Towards Usage-Based Fuzz Testing

In this paper, we want to discuss a new approach for fuzzing that combines it with usage-based testing. The new approach shall resolve some of the efficiency problems of existing fuzzing techniques. The underlying assumption of our approach is that system execution of the users unveils faults, similar to functional testing. Therefore, most remaining faults in a system should be located in parts of the system that are not regularly executed by the users and thus, little tested. From this, we conclude that the same should be true for security-relevant bugs. Normally, usage-based testing generates test cases for the most used parts of a system, in terms of both functionality and data. For the purpose of finding security weaknesses, we plan to invert this approach: aim the testing at seldom used functionality with rarely used data.

In our approach, we consider both data and behavioral fuzzing to perform security testing. However, the information provided by a usage profile is utilized by both fuzzing techniques differently.

3.1   Preparing the Usage Profile

As discussed, we presume a negative correlation between tested functionality and risk for a security relevant bugs. Therefore, the probabilities within the usage profile have to be inverted and normalized, which automatically means that the focus is put on rarely used functionality. However, functionality that is never used is not considered. It is required to map the usage profile to a model of the SUT, e.g., an environmental model. This allows identifying the unused functionality having the highest risk for security relevant bugs according to our assumption.

3.2   Usage-Based Data Fuzzing

For data fuzzing, the usage intensity of the inputs is of interest. We target fields where the inputs rarely varied, i.e. the usage profile provided only a small number of different or even no inputs. The probabilities provided by the usage profile can guide both the generation of a test scenario where the functionality is used as well as fuzz test data generation itself by utilizing information which values are already used by the users.

In addition, the different user inputs obtained from the usage profile can be considered in more detail. Users do not always provide valid input data for several reasons. This could happen due to mistypes, insufficiently educated users or unclear information what input is expected. The probabilities for events representing invalid data may be more reduced than those for events only representing valid user data and thus, reduce the chance that test scenarios are generated that are already covered by regular usage-based test cases that already using invalid input data. Therefore, if the same number of different input data is contained in the usage profile for a certain functionality, the events identifying invalid input would reduce the probability for corresponding test scenario generation more than events identifying valid input.

Through usage-based fuzz testing, we focus the fuzzing on seldom or never used system parts. We have two advantages in comparison to fuzzing without usage information. First, we reduce the risk of vulnerabilities in areas that are often neglected, first of all by the users, but as a side effect also by the maintenance of the software due to regular usage-based testing. Second, we reduce the computational effort for fuzzing because it is targeted on and restricted to areas that are likely to contain vulnerabilities.

3.3   Usage-Based Behavioral Fuzzing

In contrast, for the behavioral fuzzing only the usage frequency of functionality is of interest. Here, we invert the probabilities of the usage frequency, in order to fuzz the behavior around rarely used functionalities by modifying the test scenarios on message level by applying dedicated behavioral fuzzing operators [7].

4   Advantages of the Proposed Approach

We expect from the proposed approach of usage-based fuzz testing advantages with respect to two aspects:

- Reduced effort for maintenance between minor versions with respect to security testing. Between different versions of a software, usage-based testing can be employed in order to ensure that the quality of the most used functionalities achieve at a certain quality level. In addition, security testing performed with usage-based fuzz testing is complementary in terms of usage frequency because the probabilities of the usage profile are inverted. Thus, the effort to security testing can be reduced by focusing on parts that weren't intensely tested having a high risk of security-relevant bugs.
- The more significant aspect would be the advantage resulting from the degree of automation. As discussed in Sect. 2, the existing approaches for risk analysis require substantial manual effort. The approach of usage-based testing considers seldom or never used and thus, little or even not tested functionality as risk. The usage profile is obtained automatically by a usage monitor. The subsequent steps, i.e. inverting the usage profile, mapping it to a model of the SUT, considering the provided inputs with respect to validity, can also be performed automatically. As a result, the approach is completely automated in contrast to other approaches that combine security testing with risk assessment.

5   Example

The approach of usage-based fuzz testing is illustrated in the following, based on an example of a simple input dialog as depicted in Fig. 1. The input dialog consists of an edit box, an OK button, a cancel button, and a reset button that sets the value to the default value. The input box provides a default value that users may change by clicking in the input field and changing the default value to the desired one.

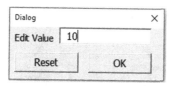

Fig. 1. Input dialog

The events that can be observed when the dialog box is opened are 'Click Edit box', 'Type Into Edit Box', 'Click OK', 'Click Reset', and 'Click X'. Additionally, two events called 'Start' and 'End' are edit that represent the events that the input dialog appears and disappears. The edges between these events represent the probabilities that the destination of an edge occurs when the source event of the edge has occurred.

Figure 2 (a) depicts the events and the probabilities based on the observed event frequencies. It should be noted that most of the users do not change the given values. In only 10 % of the cases the default value is changed by typing once in the edit box. Changes including two or more changes are even rarer.

If there are functionalities that wasn't used in no cases, these can be added by mapping the usage profile to a model of the SUT. In this example, the event 'Click Reset' was never observed, hence, it is not contained in the usage profile. By mapping the usage profile to the a model of the SUT, the missing events and corresponding edges are added. They are depicted by dashed lines in Fig. 2. The incoming and outgoing edges of the event 'Click Reset' that was not observed is therefore set to 0 %.

Given this usage profile, the one for usage-based fuzz testing can be derived by inverting the probabilities and normalizing them. The resulting usage profile is depicted in Fig. 2 (b).

Based on the inverted usage-profile, test scenarios can be generated, e.g., by random walks. Due to the inverted probabilities of the usage profile, seldom used functionality is taken into account more intensely that frequently used functionality during test scenario generation. In the given example, test scenarios would be generated where a lot of input to the edit box would be made. Through regular usage-based testing, only few different test cases would cover this functionality. Therefore, possible faults may be missed. This might pose a security risk if input validation mechanisms are incorrectly implemented or missing. Considering a functional fault detected by a functional test case. In order to fix this bug, a developer would usually perform a review of the corresponding code snippet and thus, may discover also other faults in this area and fix them. Given that a user provided invalid data, the developer would review the validation mechanism and thus, would probably find other security-relevant faults. Therefore,

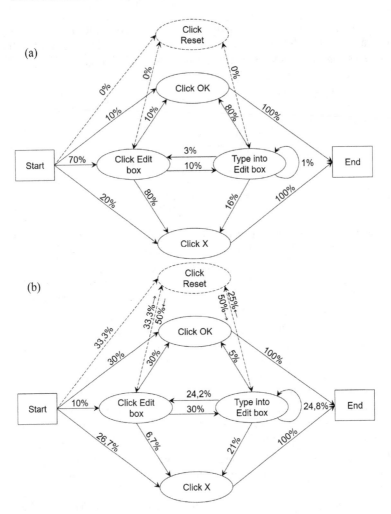

Fig. 2. (a) Usage profile including probabilities based on usage frequencies. Events that were not observed are added by mapping the usage profile to a model of the SUT. The additions were marked by dashed lines. (b) Mapped usage profile with inverted and normalized probabilities. It serves as a starting point for usage-based fuzz testing.

parts that are subject to usage-based testing may have a reduced risk to faults with respect to input validation.

Considering the seldom used functionality of changing the default value, according the usage-based testing approach, only few test cases would be generated that would cover few different inputs to the edit box. Therefore, existing faults are unlikely being detected and this is where the approach of usage-based fuzz testing comes into play. Resulting from the usage profile with inverted probabilities, test scenarios are generated that cover the typing into the edit box as depicted in Fig. 3. Usage-based data fuzzing will generate many test cases that create different malicious inputs submitted to the edit box (grey shaded in Fig. 3). Therefore, different kinds of injection vulnerabilities may be discovered having a higher chance of success due to the small number of usage-based test cases. Considering the invalid inputs provided by the usage profiles, usage-based data fuzzing is able to focus on such possible faults that were neglected by usage-based testing due to a small usage frequency. Invalid user inputs may range from values that might be out of certain range, i.e. too large or too small with respect to numbers. Those may be considered by reducing probabilities within the inverted usage profile. Utilizing this information from the usage-profile, malicious inputs covering other kind of vulnerabilities are targeted that are rarely subject of user input, such as SQL injection. The event 'Type into Edit Box' seldom occurring, therefore, usage-based data fuzzing would focus on this field, and would neglect other field even more intensely used by users. Eventually, these test cases are supplemented by those generated by usage-based behavioral fuzzing aiming at the discovery of functionality that should be disallowed.

Fig. 3. A test scenario generated from the inverted usage profile. The grey parts are the target of fuzz test data generated based on the information from the usage profile.

6   Evaluation Within the MIDAS Project

Within the MIDAS European research project [11] we are currently building a test platform on the cloud for testing of Service Oriented Architectures (SOAs). Figure 4 provides an overview of the MIDAS Platform. As part of this project, we are implementing data fuzzing, behavioral fuzzing, and usage-based testing all on the same input model. Our joint input model is a Domain Specific Language (DSL) based on Unified Modeling Language (UML) and UML Testing Profile (UTP), which already provides mechanisms for defining fuzzing operators for test cases. Moreover, the tooling for the creation of a usage profile is also developed as part of MIDAS, including usage monitoring facilities for SOA applications. The usage-based testing facilities provide the functionality to generate test cases compliant to the DSL, which can then be extended with the appropriate fuzzing operators. The presented approach of usage-based fuzz testing is achieved by an orchestration of the MIDAS test generation services for usage-based testing and fuzz testing. The tool developed for usage-based testing is called AutoQUEST [12] developed by the University of Göttingen and is integrated and improved for the MDIAS Platform. Data fuzzing within the MIDAS Platform is based on the fuzz test data generator Fuzzino [13] extended for testing web services.

Within the project, we are working together with industrial partners who supply us with both usage data as well as systems where security is a relevant property. The first system we consider comes from the health care domain and is concerned with the management of patient data, i.e., sensitive data that must be protected against adversaries. The second system we use to evaluate is a supply chain management system, where security leaks can lead to wrong orders and manipulation of databases, which can costs a lot of money, depending on the industry they are used in.

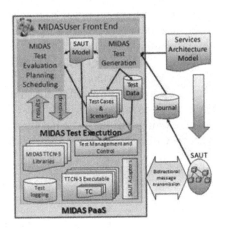

Fig. 4. Overview of the MIDAS platform.

7   Conclusion and Future Work

We propose the idea of usage-based fuzz testing, an approach that focuses data and behavioral fuzzing on rarely used and thus, little tested parts of a software. With our work in the MIDAS project, we already built a strong foundation for the implementation of such an approach. In the future, we will investigate how to best combine these techniques in order to leverage the strengths of both approaches. These investigations will include how information about data usage from the usage profile can be used to guide data fuzzing and how the test cases derived by usage-based testing can serve as foundation for behavioral fuzzing.

Acknowledgment. This work was partially funded by the EU FP 7 projects MIDAS (no. 318786) and RASEN (no. 316853).

References

1. I. E. Commission, IEC 61025 fault tree analysis (1990)
2. IEC 60812 analysis techniques for system reliability-procedure for failure mode and effects analysis (FMEA) (2006)
3. Schneier, B.: Attack trees. Dr. Dobbs J. **24**(12), 21–29 (1999)

4. Lund, M.S., Solhaug, B., Stølen, K.: The CORAS approach. Springer Science & Business Media, Heidelberg (2010)
5. Takanen, A., DeMott, J., Miller, C.: Fuzzing for Software Security Testing and Quality Assurance Ser Artech House Information Security and Privacy Series. Artech House, Boston (2008). http://books.google.de/books?id=tMuAc_y9dFYC
6. Miller, B.P., Fredriksen, L., So, B.: An empirical study of the reliability of UNIX utilities. In: Proceedings of the Workshop of Parallel and Distributed Debugging, Academic Medicine, pp. ix–xxi (1990)
7. Schneider, M., Großmann, J., Tcholtchev, N., Schieferdecker, I., Pietschker, A.: Behavioral fuzzing operators for UML sequence diagrams. In: Haugen, Ø., Reed, R., Gotzhein, R. (eds.) SAM 2012. LNCS, vol. 7744, pp. 88–104. Springer, Heidelberg (2013)
8. EC FP7 RASEN Project, FP7-316853, 2012–2015. www.rasenproject.eu
9. Herbold, S.: Usage-based Testing of Event-driven Software. Ph.D. dissertation, Dissertation, Universität Göttingen, June 2012. (electronically published on http://webdoc.sub.gwdg.de/diss/2012/herbold/)
10. Tonella, P., Ricca, F.: Statistical testing of web applications. J. Softw. Maintenance Evol. Res. Pract. **16**(1–2), 103–127 (2004)
11. EC FP7 MIDAS Project, FP7-316853, 2012–2015. www.midas-project.eu
12. Herbold, F.G.S.: Patrick Harms. Autoquest (2014). Accessed on https://autoquest.informatik.uni-goettingen.de/
13. Schneider, M.: Fuzzino (2013). Accessed on https://github.com/fraunhoferfokus/Fuzzino

Author Index

Printed in the United States
By Bookmasters